50 Honey Sweet Treat Recipes for Home

By: Kelly Johnson

Table of Contents

- Honey Almond Granola Bars
- Honey Lavender Shortbread Cookies
- Honey Yogurt Parfait with Fresh Berries
- Honey Glazed Carrots (for a sweet side treat)
- Honey Lemonade Popsicles
- Honey Roasted Nuts
- Honey Apple Cake
- Honey Cinnamon Rolls
- Honey Vanilla Ice Cream
- Honey Gingerbread Cookies
- Honey Pistachio Baklava
- Honey Peach Sorbet
- Honey Oatmeal Cookies
- Honey Banana Bread
- Honey Nut Brittle
- Honey Orange Cupcakes
- Honey Berry Tart
- Honey Lemon Tart
- Honey Sesame Cookies
- Honey Coconut Macaroons
- Honey Walnut Cake
- Honey Almond Butter
- Honey Chocolate Truffles
- Honey Pecan Pie
- Honey Citrus Salad (with fruits and a honey drizzle)
- Honey Maple Granola
- Honey Berry Smoothie Bowl (as a sweet breakfast treat)
- Honey Mint Julep Sorbet
- Honey Ginger Tea Cake
- Honey Poached Pears
- Honey Ricotta Cheesecake
- Honey Spice Cake
- Honey Vanilla Bean Madeleines
- Honey Date Bars
- Honey Pumpkin Pie

- Honey Almond Biscotti
- Honey Apple Crisp
- Honey Lemon Meringue Pie
- Honey Rosewater Ice Cream
- Honey Cardamom Rice Pudding
- Honey Fig Jam
- Honey Plum Galette
- Honey Cranberry Sauce (as a sweet condiment)
- Honey Cherry Clafoutis
- Honey Sesame Brittle
- Honey Banana Popsicles
- Honey Pear Bread Pudding
- Honey Blueberry Pancakes
- Honey Raspberry Fool
- Honey Chocolate Chip Scones

Honey Almond Granola Bars

Ingredients:

- 2 cups old-fashioned rolled oats
- 1 cup sliced almonds
- 1/2 cup honey
- 1/4 cup unsalted butter
- 1/4 cup packed light brown sugar
- 1/2 teaspoon vanilla extract
- 1/4 teaspoon salt
- 1/2 cup chopped dried fruit (optional, such as raisins, cranberries, apricots)

Instructions:

1. Preparation: Preheat your oven to 350°F (175°C). Line a 9x9 inch baking pan with parchment paper or foil, leaving an overhang on the sides to lift the bars out later.
2. Toast Oats and Almonds: Spread the oats and almonds evenly on a baking sheet. Toast in the preheated oven for about 10 minutes, stirring occasionally, until lightly browned and fragrant. Remove from the oven and reduce the oven temperature to 300°F (150°C).
3. Combine Honey, Butter, Sugar: In a small saucepan, combine the honey, butter, brown sugar, vanilla extract, and salt over medium heat. Stir occasionally until the butter is melted and the mixture is smooth.
4. Mix Everything Together: In a large bowl, combine the toasted oats and almonds with the honey mixture. Stir well until all the dry ingredients are coated.
5. Add Dried Fruit (Optional): If using dried fruit, fold it into the oat mixture at this point.
6. Press into Pan: Transfer the mixture to the prepared baking pan. Use a spatula or the back of a spoon to press the mixture firmly and evenly into the pan.
7. Bake: Bake in the 300°F (150°C) oven for 25-30 minutes, or until golden brown around the edges.
8. Cool and Cut: Allow the bars to cool completely in the pan on a wire rack. Once cooled, use the parchment paper or foil overhang to lift the bars out of the pan. Place on a cutting board and cut into bars of your desired size and shape.
9. Store: Store the granola bars in an airtight container at room temperature for up to a week, or in the refrigerator for longer storage.

Enjoy your homemade Honey Almond Granola Bars as a delicious and nutritious snack!

Honey Lavender Shortbread Cookies

Ingredients:

- 1 cup unsalted butter, softened
- 1/2 cup honey
- 2 cups all-purpose flour
- 1/4 cup cornstarch
- 1/4 teaspoon salt
- 1 tablespoon culinary lavender buds (dried, food-grade)
- Optional: Additional culinary lavender buds for garnish

Instructions:

1. Preheat Oven: Preheat your oven to 325°F (160°C). Line baking sheets with parchment paper or silicone baking mats.
2. Prepare Lavender: In a small bowl, combine the culinary lavender buds with 1 tablespoon of honey. Let it sit while you prepare the cookie dough to infuse the honey with lavender flavor.
3. Cream Butter and Honey: In a large bowl, beat together the softened butter and remaining 7 tablespoons of honey until smooth and creamy.
4. Mix Dry Ingredients: In a separate bowl, whisk together the flour, cornstarch, and salt.
5. Combine Dough: Gradually add the flour mixture to the butter-honey mixture, mixing until combined and a soft dough forms.
6. Add Infused Honey: Strain the infused honey to remove the lavender buds. Add the infused honey to the dough and mix until evenly distributed. The dough will be slightly sticky.
7. Shape Cookies: Divide the dough into two equal portions. On a lightly floured surface, shape each portion into a log about 1 1/2 inches in diameter. If the dough is too sticky to handle, refrigerate it for 15-30 minutes until firm enough to shape.
8. Chill Dough: Wrap the logs tightly in plastic wrap and refrigerate for at least 1 hour, or until firm.
9. Slice and Bake: Remove the chilled dough logs from the refrigerator and unwrap. Using a sharp knife, slice the logs into 1/4 to 1/2 inch thick rounds. Place the cookies onto the prepared baking sheets, spacing them about 1 inch apart.
10. Optional Garnish: If desired, lightly press a few lavender buds onto the top of each cookie for decoration.
11. Bake: Bake the cookies in the preheated oven for 12-15 minutes, or until the edges are lightly golden.
12. Cool: Allow the cookies to cool on the baking sheets for 5 minutes, then transfer them to a wire rack to cool completely.
13. Enjoy: Once completely cooled, serve and enjoy your delicate and fragrant Honey Lavender Shortbread Cookies!

These cookies are perfect for tea time or any occasion where you want to impress with a unique and flavorful treat.

Honey Yogurt Parfait with Fresh Berries

Ingredients:

- 1 cup plain Greek yogurt
- 2-3 tablespoons honey (adjust to taste)
- 1 teaspoon vanilla extract (optional)
- 1 cup mixed fresh berries (such as strawberries, blueberries, raspberries)
- 1/2 cup granola (homemade or store-bought)

Instructions:

1. Prepare Yogurt Mixture:
    - In a mixing bowl, combine the Greek yogurt with honey and vanilla extract (if using). Mix well until smooth and well combined. Adjust the sweetness by adding more honey if desired.
2. Prepare Berries:
    - Wash the fresh berries thoroughly and pat them dry with a paper towel. If using strawberries, hull and slice them.
3. Assemble Parfaits:
    - In serving glasses or bowls, start by layering a spoonful of the honey yogurt mixture at the bottom.
    - Add a layer of mixed berries on top of the yogurt.
    - Sprinkle a layer of granola over the berries.
    - Repeat the layers until the glasses are filled, ending with a final layer of yogurt on top.
4. Garnish:
    - Optionally, garnish the top with a few whole berries or a drizzle of honey for decoration.
5. Serve:
    - Serve immediately as a refreshing breakfast, snack, or dessert. Enjoy your delicious Honey Yogurt Parfait with Fresh Berries!

This parfait is not only delicious but also packed with protein, fiber, and antioxidants from the berries, making it a nutritious choice for any time of day. Adjust the ingredients and proportions based on your preferences and enjoy!

Honey Glazed Carrots (for a sweet side treat)

Ingredients:

- 1 cup plain Greek yogurt
- 2-3 tablespoons honey (adjust to taste)
- 1 teaspoon vanilla extract (optional)
- 1 cup mixed fresh berries (such as strawberries, blueberries, raspberries)
- 1/2 cup granola (homemade or store-bought)

Instructions:

1. Prepare Yogurt Mixture:
    - In a mixing bowl, combine the Greek yogurt with honey and vanilla extract (if using). Mix well until smooth and well combined. Adjust the sweetness by adding more honey if desired.
2. Prepare Berries:
    - Wash the fresh berries thoroughly and pat them dry with a paper towel. If using strawberries, hull and slice them.
3. Assemble Parfaits:
    - In serving glasses or bowls, start by layering a spoonful of the honey yogurt mixture at the bottom.
    - Add a layer of mixed berries on top of the yogurt.
    - Sprinkle a layer of granola over the berries.
    - Repeat the layers until the glasses are filled, ending with a final layer of yogurt on top.
4. Garnish:
    - Optionally, garnish the top with a few whole berries or a drizzle of honey for decoration.
5. Serve:
    - Serve immediately as a refreshing breakfast, snack, or dessert. Enjoy your delicious Honey Yogurt Parfait with Fresh Berries!

This parfait is not only delicious but also packed with protein, fiber, and antioxidants from the berries, making it a nutritious choice for any time of day. Adjust the ingredients and proportions based on your preferences and enjoy!

Honey Glazed Carrots (for a sweet side treat)

Ingredients:

- 1 lb (about 450g) carrots, peeled and sliced into 1/4-inch thick rounds or diagonally
- 2 tablespoons unsalted butter
- 2 tablespoons honey
- Salt and pepper, to taste
- Fresh parsley or chives, chopped (optional, for garnish)

Instructions:

1. Prepare Carrots:
    - Peel the carrots and slice them into rounds or diagonally, about 1/4-inch thick. Ensure they are of uniform thickness for even cooking.
2. Cook Carrots:
    - In a large skillet or saucepan, melt the butter over medium heat. Add the sliced carrots to the skillet and sauté for about 5 minutes, stirring occasionally, until they start to soften slightly.
3. Add Honey:
    - Drizzle the honey over the carrots in the skillet. Stir well to coat the carrots evenly with honey and continue to cook for another 5-7 minutes, or until the carrots are tender and glazed. Adjust the heat if necessary to prevent burning the honey.
4. Season:
    - Season the glazed carrots with salt and pepper to taste. Stir again to ensure even seasoning.
5. Garnish and Serve:
    - Optionally, garnish with chopped fresh parsley or chives for added freshness and color.
6. Serve Warm:
    - Transfer the honey glazed carrots to a serving dish and serve warm as a delightful and sweet side treat.

Enjoy these Honey Glazed Carrots alongside your favorite main dishes for a touch of sweetness and a burst of flavor! Adjust the amount of honey based on your preference for sweetness.

Honey Lemonade Popsicles

Ingredients:

- 1 cup freshly squeezed lemon juice (about 4-5 lemons)
- 1/2 cup honey (adjust to taste)
- 3 cups water
- Lemon slices (optional, for garnish)

Instructions:

1. Prepare Lemonade:
    - In a large pitcher, combine the freshly squeezed lemon juice and honey. Stir well until the honey is completely dissolved.
2. Add Water:
    - Add the water to the pitcher and stir until well mixed. Taste the mixture and adjust the sweetness by adding more honey if desired.
3. Fill Popsicle Molds:
    - Pour the lemonade mixture into popsicle molds, leaving a little space at the top for expansion as they freeze.
4. Optional Garnish:
    - If using lemon slices, add a thin slice to each popsicle mold for a decorative touch.
5. Insert Sticks and Freeze:
    - Insert the popsicle sticks into the molds. Place the molds in the freezer and freeze for at least 4-6 hours, or until completely frozen.
6. Unmold and Serve:
    - To unmold the popsicles, run warm water over the outside of the molds for a few seconds to loosen them. Gently pull out the popsicles.
7. Enjoy:
    - Serve immediately and enjoy the refreshing taste of Honey Lemonade Popsicles!

These popsicles are perfect for hot summer days or whenever you need a cool, sweet treat. Adjust the amount of honey based on your preference for sweetness.

Honey Roasted Nuts

Ingredients:

- 2 cups mixed nuts (such as almonds, cashews, pecans, walnuts)
- 3 tablespoons honey
- 2 tablespoons unsalted butter
- 1/2 teaspoon salt
- 1/4 teaspoon cinnamon (optional)
- 1/4 teaspoon cayenne pepper (optional, for a spicy kick)

Instructions:

1. Preheat Oven:
    - Preheat your oven to 350°F (175°C). Line a baking sheet with parchment paper or a silicone baking mat.
2. Melt Butter and Honey:
    - In a small saucepan, melt the butter over low heat. Add the honey and stir until well combined and smooth. Remove from heat.
3. Combine Nuts and Honey Mixture:
    - In a large bowl, place the mixed nuts. Pour the honey-butter mixture over the nuts and stir well to coat them evenly.
4. Add Seasonings:
    - Sprinkle the salt, and if using, the cinnamon and cayenne pepper over the coated nuts. Stir again to ensure the seasonings are evenly distributed.
5. Spread on Baking Sheet:
    - Spread the nuts in a single layer on the prepared baking sheet.
6. Roast Nuts:
    - Roast in the preheated oven for 15-20 minutes, stirring once or twice during baking to ensure even toasting. Keep a close eye on them to prevent burning.
7. Cool:
    - Remove the baking sheet from the oven and allow the nuts to cool completely on the baking sheet. They will become crisp as they cool.
8. Store:
    - Once cooled, transfer the honey roasted nuts to an airtight container. They can be stored at room temperature for up to two weeks.

Enjoy your sweet and crunchy Honey Roasted Nuts as a delicious snack or a topping for salads and desserts!

Honey Apple Cake

Ingredients:

- 2 cups all-purpose flour
- 1 1/2 teaspoons baking powder
- 1/2 teaspoon baking soda
- 1/2 teaspoon salt
- 1 teaspoon ground cinnamon
- 1/2 teaspoon ground nutmeg
- 1/2 cup unsalted butter, softened
- 1 cup honey
- 2 large eggs
- 1 teaspoon vanilla extract
- 1/2 cup plain Greek yogurt or sour cream
- 2 cups peeled and finely chopped apples (about 2 medium apples)
- 1/2 cup chopped walnuts or pecans (optional)
- Powdered sugar (optional, for dusting)

Instructions:

1. Preheat Oven:
    - Preheat your oven to 350°F (175°C). Grease and flour a 9-inch round or square baking pan.
2. Prepare Dry Ingredients:
    - In a medium bowl, whisk together the flour, baking powder, baking soda, salt, cinnamon, and nutmeg. Set aside.
3. Cream Butter and Honey:
    - In a large bowl, beat the softened butter and honey together until light and fluffy.
4. Add Eggs and Vanilla:
    - Beat in the eggs one at a time, then add the vanilla extract, mixing until well combined.
5. Combine Wet and Dry Ingredients:
    - Gradually add the dry ingredients to the wet mixture, alternating with the Greek yogurt (or sour cream), beginning and ending with the dry ingredients. Mix until just combined.
6. Fold in Apples and Nuts:
    - Gently fold in the chopped apples and nuts (if using) until evenly distributed throughout the batter.
7. Bake:
    - Pour the batter into the prepared baking pan and spread it evenly. Bake in the preheated oven for 40-50 minutes, or until a toothpick inserted into the center comes out clean.
8. Cool:

- Allow the cake to cool in the pan for about 10 minutes, then transfer it to a wire rack to cool completely.
9. Optional Dusting:
    - Once cooled, dust the top of the cake with powdered sugar, if desired.
10. Serve:
- Slice and serve your Honey Apple Cake. Enjoy!

This cake is moist, flavorful, and perfect for any occasion. The combination of honey and apples gives it a natural sweetness and a delightful texture.

Honey Cinnamon Rolls

Ingredients:

For the Dough:

- 3 1/2 to 4 cups all-purpose flour
- 1 packet (2 1/4 tsp) active dry yeast
- 1 cup milk
- 1/3 cup unsalted butter
- 1/3 cup honey
- 1/2 teaspoon salt
- 2 large eggs

For the Filling:

- 1/2 cup unsalted butter, softened
- 1/2 cup honey
- 2 tablespoons ground cinnamon
- 1/4 cup brown sugar (optional, for added sweetness)

For the Glaze:

- 1 cup powdered sugar
- 2 tablespoons honey
- 2-3 tablespoons milk or cream
- 1/2 teaspoon vanilla extract (optional)

Instructions:

1. Prepare the Dough:
    - In a small saucepan, heat the milk, butter, and honey over medium heat until the butter is melted and the mixture is warm (about 110°F/43°C). Do not boil.
    - In a large mixing bowl, combine 2 cups of flour and the yeast.
    - Add the warm milk mixture to the flour mixture. Add the eggs and salt, and beat with a mixer on low speed for 1 minute, then on medium speed for 3 minutes. Gradually add the remaining flour until a soft dough forms.
    - Turn the dough out onto a lightly floured surface and knead for about 5-7 minutes, or until the dough is smooth and elastic. Place the dough in a greased bowl, cover, and let rise in a warm place until doubled in size, about 1 to 1.5 hours.
2. Prepare the Filling:
    - In a small bowl, mix together the softened butter, honey, cinnamon, and brown sugar (if using) until well combined.
3. Assemble the Rolls:

- Punch down the risen dough and turn it out onto a lightly floured surface. Roll it into a 15x10 inch rectangle.
- Spread the honey cinnamon filling evenly over the dough.
- Starting from a long side, tightly roll up the dough into a log and pinch the seam to seal. Cut the log into 12 equal pieces and place them cut-side up in a greased 9x13 inch baking dish.

4. Second Rise:
   - Cover the dish with a clean towel and let the rolls rise in a warm place until doubled in size, about 30-45 minutes.
5. Bake:
   - Preheat your oven to 350°F (175°C). Bake the rolls for 25-30 minutes, or until they are golden brown and cooked through.
6. Prepare the Glaze:
   - In a small bowl, whisk together the powdered sugar, honey, milk (or cream), and vanilla extract (if using) until smooth. Adjust the consistency by adding more milk if needed.
7. Glaze the Rolls:
   - Let the baked rolls cool for about 10 minutes, then drizzle the glaze over the warm rolls.
8. Serve:
   - Serve the honey cinnamon rolls warm and enjoy!

These honey cinnamon rolls are perfect for breakfast, brunch, or a sweet treat any time of day. The honey adds a wonderful depth of flavor to both the dough and the filling, making them irresistible.

Honey Vanilla Ice Cream

Ingredients:

- 2 cups heavy cream
- 1 cup whole milk
- 2/3 cup honey
- 1 vanilla bean (or 2 teaspoons vanilla extract)
- 5 large egg yolks
- Pinch of salt

Instructions:

1. Prepare the Vanilla Bean:
    - If using a vanilla bean, split it lengthwise with a sharp knife and scrape out the seeds. Combine the seeds and the pod with the cream and milk in a medium saucepan.
2. Heat the Milk and Cream:
    - Add the honey to the saucepan with the cream and milk mixture. Heat over medium heat, stirring occasionally, until the mixture is hot but not boiling (about 175°F or 80°C). If using vanilla extract, add it after heating.
3. Temper the Egg Yolks:
    - In a separate bowl, whisk the egg yolks until smooth. Gradually pour about 1 cup of the hot cream mixture into the yolks, whisking constantly to prevent the eggs from cooking.
4. Cook the Custard:
    - Pour the tempered egg yolk mixture back into the saucepan with the remaining cream mixture. Cook over medium-low heat, stirring constantly with a wooden spoon or a heatproof spatula, until the mixture thickens enough to coat the back of the spoon (about 170°F or 77°C). Do not let it boil.
5. Strain and Cool:
    - Remove the saucepan from the heat and strain the custard through a fine-mesh sieve into a clean bowl to remove the vanilla bean pod and any cooked egg bits. Add a pinch of salt and stir to combine.
6. Chill the Mixture:
    - Allow the custard to cool to room temperature, then cover and refrigerate for at least 4 hours or overnight, until completely chilled.
7. Churn the Ice Cream:
    - Pour the chilled custard into an ice cream maker and churn according to the manufacturer's instructions until it reaches a soft-serve consistency.
8. Freeze the Ice Cream:
    - Transfer the churned ice cream to an airtight container and freeze for at least 2 hours, or until firm.
9. Serve:
    - Scoop and serve your homemade Honey Vanilla Ice Cream. Enjoy!

This Honey Vanilla Ice Cream is rich and creamy with a perfect balance of honey and vanilla flavors. It's a wonderful treat on its own or served with your favorite desserts.

Honey Gingerbread Cookies

Ingredients:

- 3 cups all-purpose flour
- 1 teaspoon baking soda
- 1/2 teaspoon salt
- 2 teaspoons ground ginger
- 1 teaspoon ground cinnamon
- 1/4 teaspoon ground cloves
- 1/4 teaspoon ground nutmeg
- 1/2 cup unsalted butter, softened
- 1/2 cup brown sugar, packed
- 1 large egg
- 3/4 cup honey
- 1 teaspoon vanilla extract

Instructions:

1. Prepare Dry Ingredients:
    - In a medium bowl, whisk together the flour, baking soda, salt, ginger, cinnamon, cloves, and nutmeg. Set aside.
2. Cream Butter and Sugar:
    - In a large bowl, beat the softened butter and brown sugar together until light and fluffy, about 2-3 minutes.
3. Add Wet Ingredients:
    - Beat in the egg, honey, and vanilla extract until well combined.
4. Combine Wet and Dry Ingredients:
    - Gradually add the dry ingredients to the wet mixture, mixing until just combined. The dough will be slightly sticky.
5. Chill the Dough:
    - Divide the dough in half and shape each half into a disk. Wrap each disk in plastic wrap and refrigerate for at least 2 hours or until firm. You can also chill the dough overnight.
6. Preheat Oven:
    - Preheat your oven to 350°F (175°C). Line baking sheets with parchment paper or silicone baking mats.
7. Roll Out the Dough:
    - On a lightly floured surface, roll out one disk of dough to about 1/4 inch thickness. Keep the other disk in the refrigerator until ready to use.
8. Cut Out Cookies:
    - Use cookie cutters to cut out desired shapes and place them onto the prepared baking sheets, about 1 inch apart.
9. Bake:

- Bake in the preheated oven for 8-10 minutes, or until the edges are just starting to brown. Keep an eye on them to avoid over-baking.
10. Cool:
    - Allow the cookies to cool on the baking sheets for 5 minutes, then transfer them to a wire rack to cool completely.
11. Optional Decoration:
    - Once the cookies are completely cooled, you can decorate them with royal icing, sprinkles, or any other desired decorations.
12. Serve:
    - Enjoy your Honey Gingerbread Cookies with a cup of tea or as a festive treat!

These cookies are perfect for the holiday season or any time you crave a spiced sweet treat. The honey adds a wonderful depth of flavor to the classic gingerbread taste.

Honey Pistachio Baklava

Ingredients:

For the Baklava:

- 1 package (16 oz) phyllo dough, thawed
- 2 cups unsalted pistachios, finely chopped
- 1 cup unsalted butter, melted
- 1 teaspoon ground cinnamon

For the Honey Syrup:

- 1 cup water
- 1 cup sugar
- 1 cup honey
- 1 tablespoon lemon juice
- 1 teaspoon vanilla extract
- 1 cinnamon stick

Instructions:

1. Prepare the Nut Filling:
   - In a medium bowl, combine the finely chopped pistachios and ground cinnamon. Set aside.
2. Preheat Oven:
   - Preheat your oven to 350°F (175°C). Butter a 9x13 inch baking dish.
3. Assemble the Baklava:
   - Unroll the phyllo dough and cut the whole stack to fit your baking dish. Cover the phyllo with a damp cloth to keep it from drying out as you work.
   - Place one sheet of phyllo in the bottom of the prepared baking dish and brush with melted butter. Repeat this process, layering and buttering each sheet, until you have 8 sheets layered.
   - Sprinkle a thin layer of the pistachio mixture over the top.
   - Continue layering 8 sheets of phyllo, brushing each with melted butter, followed by a layer of the pistachio mixture, until you use up all the nuts. Top with the remaining phyllo sheets, again brushing each with melted butter. Be sure to brush the top layer generously with butter.
4. Cut the Baklava:
   - Using a sharp knife, cut the baklava into diamond or square shapes, cutting all the way through to the bottom of the dish.
5. Bake:
   - Bake in the preheated oven for 45-50 minutes, or until the baklava is golden brown and crisp.
6. Prepare the Honey Syrup:

- While the baklava is baking, combine the water and sugar in a medium saucepan over medium heat. Stir until the sugar is dissolved.
- Add the honey, lemon juice, vanilla extract, and cinnamon stick. Bring to a boil, then reduce the heat and let it simmer for about 10 minutes.
- Remove from heat and let the syrup cool slightly. Remove the cinnamon stick.
7. Pour Syrup over Baklava:
    - Remove the baklava from the oven and immediately pour the hot honey syrup evenly over the hot baklava. Make sure to get the syrup into all the cuts and edges.
8. Cool and Serve:
    - Allow the baklava to cool completely, uncovered, for several hours or overnight. This helps it set and allows the syrup to be fully absorbed.
    - Once cooled, the baklava is ready to be served.

Enjoy your delicious Honey Pistachio Baklava, a perfect blend of crispy, sweet, and nutty flavors!

Honey Peach Sorbet

Ingredients:

- 4 cups ripe peaches, peeled and sliced (about 5-6 peaches)
- 1/2 cup honey (adjust to taste)
- 1/4 cup water
- 1 tablespoon lemon juice

Instructions:

1. Prepare the Peaches:
   - Peel and slice the peaches. If your peaches are very ripe, you may not need to peel them.
2. Blend the Ingredients:
   - In a blender or food processor, combine the sliced peaches, honey, water, and lemon juice. Blend until the mixture is smooth.
3. Adjust Sweetness:
   - Taste the mixture and adjust the sweetness by adding more honey if desired. Keep in mind that the sorbet will taste less sweet once it's frozen.
4. Chill the Mixture:
   - Pour the peach mixture into a large bowl and refrigerate for at least 1 hour, or until well chilled.
5. Churn the Sorbet:
   - Pour the chilled mixture into an ice cream maker and churn according to the manufacturer's instructions, usually about 20-25 minutes, until it reaches a soft-serve consistency.
6. Freeze the Sorbet:
   - Transfer the churned sorbet to an airtight container. Press a piece of plastic wrap directly onto the surface of the sorbet to prevent ice crystals from forming. Freeze for at least 2 hours, or until firm.
7. Serve:
   - Scoop and serve the Honey Peach Sorbet. Enjoy!

This Honey Peach Sorbet is a perfect way to enjoy the natural sweetness of summer peaches with a hint of honey. It's a refreshing and healthy treat for hot days!

Honey Oatmeal Cookies

Ingredients:

- 1 cup unsalted butter, softened
- 1 cup honey
- 1/2 cup brown sugar, packed
- 2 large eggs
- 1 teaspoon vanilla extract
- 1 1/2 cups all-purpose flour
- 1 teaspoon baking soda
- 1 teaspoon ground cinnamon
- 1/2 teaspoon salt
- 3 cups old-fashioned rolled oats
- 1 cup raisins or chocolate chips (optional)
- 1/2 cup chopped nuts (optional)

Instructions:

1. Preheat Oven:
    - Preheat your oven to 350°F (175°C). Line baking sheets with parchment paper or silicone baking mats.
2. Cream Butter and Sweeteners:
    - In a large bowl, beat the softened butter, honey, and brown sugar together until light and fluffy.
3. Add Eggs and Vanilla:
    - Beat in the eggs one at a time, then add the vanilla extract, mixing until well combined.
4. Mix Dry Ingredients:
    - In a separate bowl, whisk together the flour, baking soda, cinnamon, and salt.
5. Combine Wet and Dry Ingredients:
    - Gradually add the dry ingredients to the wet mixture, mixing until just combined.
6. Add Oats and Optional Mix-Ins:
    - Stir in the rolled oats, and if using, add raisins or chocolate chips and chopped nuts.
7. Scoop and Bake:
    - Drop rounded tablespoons of dough onto the prepared baking sheets, spacing them about 2 inches apart. Flatten each cookie slightly with the back of a spoon or your hand.
    - Bake in the preheated oven for 10-12 minutes, or until the edges are golden brown and the centers are set.
8. Cool:
    - Allow the cookies to cool on the baking sheets for 5 minutes, then transfer them to a wire rack to cool completely.
9. Serve:

- Enjoy your Honey Oatmeal Cookies with a glass of milk or a cup of tea!

These cookies are soft, chewy, and filled with the natural sweetness of honey. The oats add a hearty texture, making them a perfect treat for any time of the day.

Honey Banana Bread

Ingredients:

- 1/2 cup unsalted butter, melted
- 1/2 cup honey
- 2 large eggs
- 1 teaspoon vanilla extract
- 1 cup mashed ripe bananas (about 2-3 bananas)
- 1/4 cup plain Greek yogurt or sour cream
- 1 3/4 cups all-purpose flour
- 1 teaspoon baking soda
- 1/2 teaspoon salt
- 1 teaspoon ground cinnamon
- 1/2 cup chopped nuts or chocolate chips (optional)

Instructions:

1. Preheat Oven:
   - Preheat your oven to 350°F (175°C). Grease a 9x5 inch loaf pan or line it with parchment paper.
2. Mix Wet Ingredients:
   - In a large bowl, whisk together the melted butter and honey until well combined.
   - Add the eggs and vanilla extract, and whisk until smooth.
   - Stir in the mashed bananas and Greek yogurt (or sour cream) until well combined.
3. Combine Dry Ingredients:
   - In a separate bowl, whisk together the flour, baking soda, salt, and ground cinnamon.
4. Combine Wet and Dry Ingredients:
   - Gradually add the dry ingredients to the wet mixture, stirring until just combined. Do not overmix.
   - If using, fold in the chopped nuts or chocolate chips.
5. Pour into Pan:
   - Pour the batter into the prepared loaf pan and spread it evenly.
6. Bake:
   - Bake in the preheated oven for 50-60 minutes, or until a toothpick inserted into the center of the bread comes out clean.
   - If the top starts to brown too quickly, tent the loaf with aluminum foil.
7. Cool:
   - Allow the banana bread to cool in the pan for about 10 minutes, then transfer it to a wire rack to cool completely.
8. Serve:
   - Slice and serve your Honey Banana Bread. Enjoy!

This Honey Banana Bread is moist, flavorful, and naturally sweetened with honey. It's perfect for breakfast, a snack, or dessert.

Honey Nut Brittle

Ingredients:

- 1 cup granulated sugar
- 1/2 cup honey
- 1/4 cup water
- 1/4 teaspoon salt
- 1 cup mixed nuts (such as almonds, peanuts, walnuts, etc.)
- 1 tablespoon unsalted butter
- 1 teaspoon vanilla extract
- 1/2 teaspoon baking soda

Instructions:

1. Prepare Baking Sheet:
    - Line a baking sheet with parchment paper or a silicone baking mat. Set aside.
2. Toast the Nuts (Optional):
    - If desired, toast the nuts in a dry skillet over medium heat for a few minutes until lightly browned and fragrant. Remove from heat and set aside.
3. Make the Brittle:
    - In a medium saucepan, combine the sugar, honey, water, and salt. Stir over medium heat until the sugar is dissolved.
4. Cook to Soft Crack Stage:
    - Insert a candy thermometer into the mixture and bring it to a boil without stirring. Cook until the mixture reaches 290°F (143°C), also known as the soft-crack stage.
5. Add Nuts and Butter:
    - Once the mixture reaches 290°F (143°C), stir in the nuts and butter. Cook, stirring constantly, until the mixture reaches 300°F (149°C), which is the hard-crack stage. The mixture should be a golden amber color.
6. Remove from Heat:
    - Remove the saucepan from the heat and quickly stir in the vanilla extract and baking soda. The mixture will bubble up vigorously.
7. Pour and Spread:
    - Immediately pour the hot mixture onto the prepared baking sheet. Use a spatula or the back of a spoon to spread it into an even layer, about 1/4 inch thick.
8. Cool and Break:
    - Let the brittle cool completely at room temperature until hardened, about 30 minutes to 1 hour. Once completely cooled and hardened, break the brittle into pieces using your hands or a knife.
9. Store:
    - Store the Honey Nut Brittle in an airtight container at room temperature. It can keep well for up to 2 weeks.

Enjoy your homemade Honey Nut Brittle as a sweet and crunchy snack or give it as a delightful homemade gift! Adjust the types of nuts used according to your preference.

Honey Orange Cupcakes

Ingredients:

For the Cupcakes:

- 1 3/4 cups all-purpose flour
- 1 teaspoon baking powder
- 1/2 teaspoon baking soda
- 1/4 teaspoon salt
- Zest of 1 orange
- 1/2 cup unsalted butter, softened
- 3/4 cup honey
- 2 large eggs
- 1/2 cup freshly squeezed orange juice
- 1/4 cup buttermilk (or substitute with milk + 1 teaspoon vinegar)

For the Honey Orange Glaze:

- 1 cup powdered sugar
- 2 tablespoons honey
- 2-3 tablespoons freshly squeezed orange juice

Instructions:

1. Preheat Oven:
    - Preheat your oven to 350°F (175°C). Line a muffin tin with paper cupcake liners.
2. Prepare Dry Ingredients:
    - In a medium bowl, whisk together the flour, baking powder, baking soda, salt, and orange zest. Set aside.
3. Cream Butter and Honey:
    - In a large bowl, cream together the softened butter and honey until light and fluffy.
4. Add Eggs:
    - Add the eggs one at a time, mixing well after each addition.
5. Combine Wet and Dry Ingredients:
    - Alternately add the dry ingredients and the orange juice to the butter mixture, beginning and ending with the dry ingredients. Mix until just combined.
6. Add Buttermilk:
    - Stir in the buttermilk until smooth.
7. Fill Cupcake Liners:
    - Divide the batter evenly among the prepared cupcake liners, filling each about 2/3 full.
8. Bake:

- Bake in the preheated oven for 18-20 minutes, or until a toothpick inserted into the center of a cupcake comes out clean.
9. Cool:
    - Remove the cupcakes from the muffin tin and place them on a wire rack to cool completely.
10. Prepare the Glaze:
    - In a small bowl, whisk together the powdered sugar, honey, and orange juice until smooth and combined. Adjust the consistency by adding more orange juice if needed.
11. Glaze the Cupcakes:
    - Once the cupcakes are completely cooled, drizzle the honey orange glaze over the tops of the cupcakes.
12. Serve:
    - Allow the glaze to set for a few minutes before serving.

These Honey Orange Cupcakes are moist, fragrant, and bursting with citrus flavor. They make a wonderful treat for any occasion, from afternoon tea to dessert after dinner. Enjoy!

Honey Berry Tart

Ingredients:

For the Tart Crust:

- 1 1/2 cups all-purpose flour
- 1/4 cup granulated sugar
- 1/4 teaspoon salt
- 1/2 cup unsalted butter, cold and cut into small cubes
- 1 large egg yolk
- 2-3 tablespoons ice water

For the Honey Mascarpone Filling:

- 8 oz mascarpone cheese, softened
- 1/4 cup honey
- 1 teaspoon vanilla extract

For the Berry Topping:

- 2 cups mixed berries (such as strawberries, blueberries, raspberries, blackberries)
- 2 tablespoons honey (for drizzling)
- Fresh mint leaves, for garnish (optional)

Instructions:

1. Make the Tart Crust:
    - In a food processor, combine the flour, sugar, and salt. Pulse a few times to mix.
    - Add the cold cubed butter and pulse until the mixture resembles coarse crumbs.
    - Add the egg yolk and pulse until the dough starts to come together. If needed, add ice water, 1 tablespoon at a time, until the dough forms into a ball.
    - Flatten the dough into a disk, wrap it in plastic wrap, and refrigerate for at least 30 minutes.
2. Preheat Oven and Prepare Tart Pan:
    - Preheat your oven to 375°F (190°C). Lightly grease a 9-inch tart pan with a removable bottom.
3. Roll out and Bake the Tart Crust:
    - On a lightly floured surface, roll out the chilled dough into a circle about 12 inches in diameter and 1/8 inch thick.
    - Carefully transfer the dough to the prepared tart pan, pressing it into the bottom and sides. Trim any excess dough from the edges.
    - Prick the bottom of the crust with a fork. Line the crust with parchment paper or foil and fill it with pie weights or dried beans.

- Bake in the preheated oven for 15 minutes. Remove the weights and parchment paper, then bake for an additional 10-12 minutes, or until the crust is golden brown. Allow the crust to cool completely in the pan on a wire rack.
4. Prepare the Honey Mascarpone Filling:
    - In a medium bowl, whisk together the softened mascarpone cheese, honey, and vanilla extract until smooth and well combined.
5. Assemble the Tart:
    - Spread the honey mascarpone filling evenly over the cooled tart crust.
6. Arrange the Berries:
    - Arrange the mixed berries over the top of the mascarpone filling in a decorative pattern.
7. Drizzle with Honey:
    - Drizzle the 2 tablespoons of honey evenly over the berries.
8. Chill and Serve:
    - Chill the tart in the refrigerator for at least 1 hour before serving to allow the filling to set.
    - Garnish with fresh mint leaves, if desired, before serving.

This Honey Berry Tart is a beautiful and delicious dessert that showcases the natural sweetness of honey and the freshness of summer berries. It's perfect for any special occasion or as a delightful treat for family and friends. Enjoy!

Honey Lemon Tart

Ingredients:

For the Tart Crust:

- 1 1/2 cups all-purpose flour
- 1/4 cup granulated sugar
- 1/4 teaspoon salt
- 1/2 cup unsalted butter, cold and cut into small cubes
- 1 large egg yolk
- 2-3 tablespoons ice water

For the Lemon Curd Filling:

- 3/4 cup fresh lemon juice (about 4-5 lemons)
- Zest of 2 lemons
- 1 cup granulated sugar
- 1/2 cup honey
- 1/2 cup unsalted butter, cubed
- 4 large eggs
- 2 large egg yolks
- Pinch of salt

Instructions:

1. Make the Tart Crust:
    - In a food processor, combine the flour, sugar, and salt. Pulse a few times to mix.
    - Add the cold cubed butter and pulse until the mixture resembles coarse crumbs.
    - Add the egg yolk and pulse until the dough starts to come together. If needed, add ice water, 1 tablespoon at a time, until the dough forms into a ball.
    - Flatten the dough into a disk, wrap it in plastic wrap, and refrigerate for at least 30 minutes.
2. Preheat Oven and Prepare Tart Pan:
    - Preheat your oven to 375°F (190°C). Lightly grease a 9-inch tart pan with a removable bottom.
3. Roll out and Bake the Tart Crust:
    - On a lightly floured surface, roll out the chilled dough into a circle about 12 inches in diameter and 1/8 inch thick.
    - Carefully transfer the dough to the prepared tart pan, pressing it into the bottom and sides. Trim any excess dough from the edges.
    - Prick the bottom of the crust with a fork. Line the crust with parchment paper or foil and fill it with pie weights or dried beans.

- Bake in the preheated oven for 15 minutes. Remove the weights and parchment paper, then bake for an additional 10-12 minutes, or until the crust is golden brown. Allow the crust to cool completely in the pan on a wire rack.
4. Make the Lemon Curd Filling:
    - In a medium saucepan, combine the lemon juice, lemon zest, granulated sugar, honey, and cubed butter. Heat over medium heat, stirring constantly, until the butter is melted and the mixture is smooth and hot (do not boil).
    - In a separate bowl, whisk together the eggs, egg yolks, and pinch of salt until well combined.
    - Gradually whisk the hot lemon mixture into the egg mixture, a little at a time, to temper the eggs.
5. Cook the Lemon Curd:
    - Return the combined mixture to the saucepan. Cook over medium-low heat, stirring constantly with a wooden spoon or heatproof spatula, until the mixture thickens and coats the back of the spoon, about 5-7 minutes. Do not let it boil.
6. Strain the Lemon Curd:
    - Remove the saucepan from the heat and strain the lemon curd through a fine-mesh sieve into a clean bowl to remove any zest or cooked bits of egg.
7. Assemble the Tart:
    - Pour the strained lemon curd into the cooled tart crust, spreading it evenly with a spatula.
8. Chill and Serve:
    - Chill the tart in the refrigerator for at least 2 hours, or until set.
    - Optionally, garnish with whipped cream, fresh berries, or dust with powdered sugar before serving.

This Honey Lemon Tart is tangy, sweet, and perfect for citrus lovers. The honey adds a delightful depth of flavor to the bright lemony filling. Enjoy this tart as a refreshing dessert or a special treat for any occasion!

Honey Sesame Cookies

Ingredients:

- 1/2 cup unsalted butter, softened
- 1/2 cup honey
- 1/2 cup granulated sugar
- 1 large egg
- 1 teaspoon vanilla extract
- 2 cups all-purpose flour
- 1 teaspoon baking powder
- 1/4 teaspoon salt
- 1/2 cup sesame seeds (toasted, if preferred)
- Additional sesame seeds for rolling (optional)

Instructions:

1. Preheat Oven:
   - Preheat your oven to 350°F (175°C). Line baking sheets with parchment paper.
2. Cream Butter, Honey, and Sugar:
   - In a large bowl, cream together the softened butter, honey, and granulated sugar until light and fluffy.
3. Add Egg and Vanilla:
   - Beat in the egg and vanilla extract until well combined.
4. Mix Dry Ingredients:
   - In a separate bowl, whisk together the flour, baking powder, and salt.
5. Combine Wet and Dry Ingredients:
   - Gradually add the dry ingredients to the wet mixture, mixing until just combined.
6. Add Sesame Seeds:
   - Stir in the sesame seeds until evenly distributed throughout the dough.
7. Form Dough Balls:
   - Optional: Roll tablespoon-sized portions of dough into balls and then roll them in additional sesame seeds for a more pronounced sesame flavor and texture.
8. Bake:
   - Place the dough balls onto the prepared baking sheets, spacing them about 2 inches apart.
9. Flatten Cookies (Optional):
   - Flatten each dough ball slightly with the back of a spoon or your fingers for a more uniform shape.
10. Bake:
    - Bake in the preheated oven for 10-12 minutes, or until the edges are golden brown.
11. Cool:
    - Allow the cookies to cool on the baking sheets for 5 minutes, then transfer them to a wire rack to cool completely.

12. Serve:
    - Enjoy your delicious Honey Sesame Cookies with a cup of tea or coffee!

These cookies have a lovely balance of sweetness from honey and a nutty crunch from toasted sesame seeds. They make a delightful treat for any occasion and are sure to be enjoyed by everyone!

Honey Coconut Macaroons

Ingredients:

- 3 cups sweetened shredded coconut
- 1/2 cup honey
- 2 large egg whites
- 1/4 teaspoon salt
- 1/2 teaspoon vanilla extract

Instructions:

1. Preheat Oven:
    - Preheat your oven to 325°F (160°C). Line a baking sheet with parchment paper or a silicone baking mat.
2. Mix Ingredients:
    - In a large bowl, combine the shredded coconut, honey, egg whites, salt, and vanilla extract. Stir well until all ingredients are thoroughly combined and the coconut is evenly coated.
3. Form Macaroons:
    - Using a spoon or a small cookie scoop, portion the mixture and shape it into small mounds, about 1 to 1.5 inches in diameter. You can use your hands to compact the mixture slightly if needed.
4. Bake:
    - Place the formed macaroons onto the prepared baking sheet, spacing them about 1 inch apart.
5. **Bake in the preheated oven for 20-25 minutes, or until the edges and tops of the macaroons are golden brown.
6. Cool:
    - Allow the macaroons to cool on the baking sheet for about 5 minutes, then transfer them to a wire rack to cool completely.
7. Serve:
    - Enjoy your delicious Honey Coconut Macaroons! They are perfect as a sweet snack or dessert.

These macaroons are naturally sweetened with honey and have a wonderful chewy texture from the coconut. They are easy to make and are sure to be a hit with coconut lovers!

Honey Walnut Cake

Ingredients:

For the Cake:

- 1 cup all-purpose flour
- 1 teaspoon baking powder
- 1/4 teaspoon baking soda
- 1/4 teaspoon salt
- 1/2 cup unsalted butter, softened
- 1/2 cup honey
- 2 large eggs
- 1/2 cup plain Greek yogurt (or sour cream)
- 1 teaspoon vanilla extract
- 1/2 cup chopped walnuts

For the Honey Glaze:

- 1/4 cup honey
- 2 tablespoons unsalted butter
- 1/4 cup chopped walnuts, for topping (optional)

Instructions:

1. Preheat Oven and Prepare Pan:
    - Preheat your oven to 350°F (175°C). Grease and flour a 9-inch round cake pan or line it with parchment paper.
2. Mix Dry Ingredients:
    - In a medium bowl, whisk together the flour, baking powder, baking soda, and salt. Set aside.
3. Cream Butter and Honey:
    - In a large bowl, cream together the softened butter and honey until smooth and creamy.
4. Add Eggs and Vanilla:
    - Add the eggs one at a time, beating well after each addition. Stir in the vanilla extract.
5. Alternate Mixing:
    - Gradually add the dry ingredients to the butter mixture, alternating with the Greek yogurt (or sour cream), beginning and ending with the dry ingredients. Mix until just combined.
6. Fold in Walnuts:
    - Gently fold in the chopped walnuts until evenly distributed in the batter.
7. Bake:
    - Pour the batter into the prepared cake pan and spread it evenly.

- Bake in the preheated oven for 25-30 minutes, or until a toothpick inserted into the center of the cake comes out clean.
8. **Prepare Honey Glaze:**
    - While the cake is baking, prepare the honey glaze. In a small saucepan, combine the honey and butter. Heat over medium heat, stirring constantly, until the butter is melted and the mixture is smooth.
9. **Glaze the Cake:**
    - Once the cake is baked and still warm, poke several holes in the top of the cake using a skewer or fork. Pour the warm honey glaze over the top of the cake, allowing it to soak in.
10. **Cool and Serve:**
    - Let the cake cool in the pan for 10-15 minutes. If desired, sprinkle chopped walnuts over the top for decoration.
    - Serve slices of the Honey Walnut Cake warm or at room temperature.

This Honey Walnut Cake is moist, nutty, and has a lovely honey flavor throughout. It's a perfect dessert or sweet treat, especially enjoyable with a cup of tea or coffee.

Honey Almond Butter

Ingredients:

- 2 cups almonds (raw or roasted, unsalted)
- 2-3 tablespoons honey (adjust to taste)
- 1/4 teaspoon salt (optional, adjust to taste)

Instructions:

1. Roast the Almonds (if using raw almonds):
    - Preheat your oven to 350°F (175°C). Spread the almonds in a single layer on a baking sheet.
    - Roast the almonds for 10-12 minutes, stirring occasionally, until fragrant and lightly golden. Be careful not to let them burn. Skip this step if you are using already roasted almonds.
2. Blend the Almonds:
    - Transfer the roasted almonds to a food processor or high-speed blender. If using raw almonds, you may need to let them cool slightly before blending.
    - Process the almonds for about 10-15 minutes, scraping down the sides of the processor bowl or blender as needed. Initially, the almonds will turn into a fine meal, then clump together, and eventually become creamy.
    - Be patient; the process may take some time depending on your equipment. The almonds will go through stages of grinding and then become smoother and more butter-like.
3. Add Honey and Salt:
    - Once the almonds are smooth and creamy (resembling a nut butter consistency), add the honey and salt (if using).
    - Blend again until the honey is fully incorporated into the almond butter. Taste and adjust sweetness or saltiness as desired.
4. Store:
    - Transfer the honey almond butter to a clean, airtight container, such as a glass jar. Store it in the refrigerator for up to a month.
5. Enjoy:
    - Spread honey almond butter on toast, use it as a dip for fruit, or enjoy it straight from the jar! It's deliciously sweet and nutty, perfect for various snacks and recipes.

This homemade honey almond butter is healthier than store-bought versions, as it contains no added sugars or oils apart from the natural honey and almond oils. Adjust the sweetness to your preference and enjoy the rich flavor of almonds combined with honey!

Honey Chocolate Truffles

Ingredients:

- 8 ounces (about 1 1/4 cups) semi-sweet or dark chocolate, finely chopped
- 1/2 cup heavy cream
- 2 tablespoons honey
- 1/2 teaspoon vanilla extract
- Cocoa powder, powdered sugar, finely chopped nuts, or melted chocolate for coating (optional)

Instructions:

1. Prepare the Chocolate:
   - Place the finely chopped chocolate in a heatproof bowl.
2. Heat the Cream and Honey:
   - In a small saucepan, heat the heavy cream and honey over medium heat until it just starts to simmer. Stir occasionally to ensure the honey is fully incorporated into the cream.
3. Combine and Melt:
   - Pour the hot cream mixture over the chopped chocolate. Let it sit for about 1 minute to soften the chocolate.
   - Gently stir the mixture with a spatula or whisk until the chocolate is completely melted and the mixture is smooth and shiny.
4. Add Vanilla Extract:
   - Stir in the vanilla extract until well combined.
5. Chill the Mixture:
   - Cover the bowl with plastic wrap, ensuring the plastic wrap touches the surface of the chocolate mixture to prevent a skin from forming. Chill in the refrigerator for at least 2 hours, or until the mixture is firm enough to scoop and roll into balls.
6. Shape the Truffles:
   - Once chilled, use a spoon or a small cookie scoop to portion out the chocolate mixture. Roll each portion into a smooth ball between your palms. Work quickly to prevent the mixture from melting.
7. Coat the Truffles (Optional):
   - Roll the truffles in cocoa powder, powdered sugar, finely chopped nuts, or dip them in melted chocolate. This step is optional but adds texture and flavor to the truffles.
8. Chill Again (Optional):
   - Place the coated truffles on a baking sheet lined with parchment paper and chill them in the refrigerator for another 15-20 minutes to set the coating.
9. Serve:
   - Arrange the truffles on a serving plate or in small candy cups. Serve chilled or at room temperature.
10. Storage:

- Store the Honey Chocolate Truffles in an airtight container in the refrigerator for up to 2 weeks. Bring them to room temperature before serving for the best texture and flavor.

These Honey Chocolate Truffles are rich, smooth, and indulgent with a hint of honey sweetness. They make a perfect homemade treat for special occasions or as a delightful gift for chocolate lovers. Enjoy!

Honey Pecan Pie

Ingredients:

For the Pie Crust:

- 1 1/4 cups all-purpose flour
- 1/2 teaspoon salt
- 1/2 cup unsalted butter, cold and cut into small cubes
- 3-4 tablespoons ice water

For the Filling:

- 1 cup honey
- 3/4 cup light corn syrup
- 1/4 cup unsalted butter, melted
- 3 large eggs
- 1 teaspoon vanilla extract
- 1/4 teaspoon salt
- 2 cups pecan halves

Instructions:

1. Prepare the Pie Crust:
    - In a large bowl, whisk together the flour and salt. Add the cold cubed butter.
    - Use a pastry cutter or your fingers to cut the butter into the flour mixture until it resembles coarse crumbs with some larger pea-sized pieces.
    - Gradually add ice water, 1 tablespoon at a time, mixing with a fork until the dough just begins to come together.
    - Turn the dough out onto a clean surface and gather it into a ball. Flatten into a disk, wrap in plastic wrap, and refrigerate for at least 30 minutes.
2. Preheat Oven:
    - Preheat your oven to 350°F (175°C).
3. Roll out the Pie Crust:
    - On a lightly floured surface, roll out the chilled dough into a circle about 12 inches in diameter. Transfer it to a 9-inch pie dish. Trim and crimp the edges as desired. Place the pie dish with the crust in the refrigerator while you prepare the filling.
4. Make the Filling:
    - In a medium bowl, whisk together the honey, corn syrup, melted butter, eggs, vanilla extract, and salt until well combined.
5. Add Pecans:
    - Stir in the pecan halves until they are evenly coated with the filling mixture.
6. Assemble and Bake:
    - Pour the pecan filling into the prepared pie crust.
    - Place the pie on a baking sheet to catch any potential drips during baking.

7. Bake:
    - Bake in the preheated oven for 50-60 minutes, or until the filling is set and slightly puffed, and the crust is golden brown.
8. Cool and Serve:
    - Allow the pie to cool completely on a wire rack before slicing and serving.
9. Optional:
    - Serve the Honey Pecan Pie with a dollop of whipped cream or a scoop of vanilla ice cream for a delicious dessert treat.

This Honey Pecan Pie is rich, sweet, and loaded with crunchy pecans in a luscious honey-infused filling. It's perfect for holiday gatherings or any special occasion where you want to impress with a homemade dessert. Enjoy!

Honey Citrus Salad (with fruits and a honey drizzle)

Ingredients:

For the Salad:

- 2 oranges (such as navel or blood oranges), peeled and sliced
- 2 grapefruits (pink or yellow), peeled and sliced
- 2 cups fresh strawberries, hulled and sliced
- 1 cup fresh blueberries
- 1 cup fresh raspberries
- Fresh mint leaves, for garnish (optional)

For the Honey Drizzle:

- 1/4 cup honey
- 2 tablespoons fresh lemon juice
- Zest of 1 lemon
- Zest of 1 orange

Instructions:

1. Prepare the Fruits:
    - Wash, peel (if necessary), and slice the oranges and grapefruits into rounds or segments. Hull the strawberries and slice them. Rinse the blueberries and raspberries.
2. Arrange the Salad:
    - In a large serving bowl or on a platter, arrange the sliced oranges, grapefruits, strawberries, blueberries, and raspberries in a visually appealing manner. Sprinkle some fresh mint leaves over the top for garnish if desired.
3. Make the Honey Drizzle:
    - In a small bowl, whisk together the honey, fresh lemon juice, lemon zest, and orange zest until well combined.
4. Drizzle Over the Salad:
    - Drizzle the honey mixture evenly over the arranged fruits just before serving. You can adjust the amount of honey drizzle according to your taste preference.
5. Serve:
    - Serve the Honey Citrus Salad immediately as a refreshing and light dessert or side dish. Enjoy the vibrant flavors of the fresh fruits complemented by the sweet and tangy honey drizzle.

This Honey Citrus Salad is not only delicious but also packed with vitamins and antioxidants from the colorful assortment of fruits. It's perfect for brunches, picnics, or as a healthy dessert option after a meal.

Honey Maple Granola

Ingredients:

- 3 cups old-fashioned rolled oats
- 1 cup chopped nuts (such as almonds, pecans, or walnuts)
- 1/2 cup unsweetened shredded coconut
- 1/4 cup sunflower seeds (optional)
- 1/4 cup sesame seeds (optional)
- 1/2 teaspoon ground cinnamon
- 1/4 teaspoon salt
- 1/2 cup honey
- 1/4 cup maple syrup
- 1/4 cup coconut oil, melted
- 1 teaspoon vanilla extract
- 1 cup dried fruit (such as raisins, cranberries, or chopped apricots)

Instructions:

1. Preheat Oven:
    - Preheat your oven to 300°F (150°C). Line a large baking sheet with parchment paper.
2. Mix Dry Ingredients:
    - In a large bowl, combine the rolled oats, chopped nuts, shredded coconut, sunflower seeds, sesame seeds (if using), ground cinnamon, and salt. Stir well to combine.
3. Prepare Wet Ingredients:
    - In a small saucepan, combine the honey, maple syrup, melted coconut oil, and vanilla extract. Heat over medium-low heat, stirring occasionally, until the mixture is smooth and well combined.
4. Combine and Bake:
    - Pour the honey-maple mixture over the dry ingredients in the bowl. Stir until all the dry ingredients are evenly coated with the wet mixture.
5. Bake the Granola:
    - Spread the granola mixture evenly onto the prepared baking sheet. Press it down slightly with the back of a spoon or spatula to create an even layer.
6. Bake in the preheated oven for 30-35 minutes, stirring halfway through. The granola should be golden brown and fragrant.

Honey Berry Smoothie Bowl (as a sweet breakfast treat)

Ingredients:

For the Smoothie Base:

- 1 cup frozen mixed berries (such as strawberries, blueberries, raspberries)
- 1 ripe banana, sliced and frozen
- 1/2 cup plain Greek yogurt
- 1-2 tablespoons honey (adjust to taste)
- 1/4 cup almond milk or any milk of your choice

Toppings:

- Fresh berries (sliced strawberries, blueberries, raspberries)
- Sliced banana
- Granola
- Chia seeds or flax seeds
- Honey, for drizzling
- Shredded coconut (optional)
- Nut or seed butter (optional)

Instructions:

1. Prepare the Smoothie Base:
    - In a blender, combine the frozen mixed berries, frozen banana slices, Greek yogurt, honey, and almond milk.
    - Blend until smooth and creamy, adding more almond milk if needed to reach your desired consistency. The smoothie should be thick enough to eat with a spoon.
2. Assemble the Smoothie Bowl:
    - Pour the smoothie into a bowl.
3. Add Toppings:
    - Arrange fresh berries, sliced banana, granola, and chia or flax seeds on top of the smoothie base.
    - Drizzle honey over the toppings for extra sweetness.
4. Optional Garnishes:
    - Sprinkle shredded coconut or add a dollop of nut or seed butter for added flavor and texture.
5. Serve Immediately:
    - Enjoy your Honey Berry Smoothie Bowl immediately for a delicious and nutritious breakfast treat!

This Honey Berry Smoothie Bowl is not only satisfying and delicious but also packed with antioxidants, fiber, and protein to kickstart your day. It's customizable with your favorite fruits and toppings, making it a versatile and enjoyable breakfast option.

Honey Mint Julep Sorbet

Ingredients:

- 1 cup water
- 1/2 cup honey
- 1/2 cup fresh mint leaves, tightly packed
- 1/4 cup bourbon (optional, for an adult version)
- 1/4 cup fresh lemon juice (about 2 lemons)
- Zest of 1 lemon
- Mint leaves, for garnish (optional)

Instructions:

1. Make Honey Mint Syrup:
    - In a small saucepan, combine the water, honey, and fresh mint leaves. Bring to a simmer over medium heat, stirring occasionally until the honey is dissolved.
    - Remove from heat and let the mint leaves steep in the syrup for about 10-15 minutes.
2. Strain and Chill:
    - Strain the syrup through a fine-mesh sieve into a bowl, pressing on the mint leaves to extract all the flavor. Discard the mint leaves.
    - Stir in the bourbon (if using), fresh lemon juice, and lemon zest into the syrup. Mix well.
3. Chill the Mixture:
    - Cover and refrigerate the mixture until thoroughly chilled, at least 2-3 hours or overnight.
4. Freeze in Ice Cream Maker:
    - Transfer the chilled mixture to an ice cream maker and churn according to the manufacturer's instructions until it reaches a sorbet-like consistency.
5. Serve:
    - Scoop the sorbet into serving dishes or bowls.
    - Garnish with fresh mint leaves, if desired.
    - Serve immediately as a refreshing dessert or palate cleanser.
6. Optional:
    - For a more slushy consistency, place the sorbet in the freezer for about 30 minutes before serving.

This Honey Mint Julep Sorbet offers a delightful blend of honey sweetness, fresh mint, and a hint of lemon, with the optional addition of bourbon for a sophisticated twist. It's perfect for summer gatherings or as a special treat after a meal. Enjoy!

Honey Ginger Tea Cake

Ingredients:

- 1/2 cup unsalted butter, softened
- 1/2 cup honey
- 2 large eggs
- 1/2 cup plain Greek yogurt (or sour cream)
- 1 teaspoon vanilla extract
- 1 tablespoon freshly grated ginger (or 1 teaspoon ground ginger)
- 1 1/2 cups all-purpose flour
- 1 teaspoon baking powder
- 1/2 teaspoon baking soda
- 1/4 teaspoon salt
- 1/4 cup milk (any kind)
- Zest of 1 lemon (optional, for added flavor)

For the Honey Glaze:

- 1/4 cup honey
- 1 tablespoon hot water

Instructions:

1. Preheat Oven and Prepare Pan:
    - Preheat your oven to 350°F (175°C). Grease a 9x5 inch loaf pan and line it with parchment paper for easy removal.
2. Cream Butter and Honey:
    - In a large bowl, cream together the softened butter and honey until smooth and creamy.
3. Add Eggs and Yogurt:
    - Beat in the eggs, one at a time, until well combined. Mix in the Greek yogurt (or sour cream), vanilla extract, and freshly grated ginger until smooth.
4. Combine Dry Ingredients:
    - In a separate bowl, whisk together the flour, baking powder, baking soda, and salt. If using, add the lemon zest to the dry ingredients and mix well.
5. Mix Wet and Dry Ingredients:
    - Gradually add the dry ingredients to the wet mixture, alternating with the milk, beginning and ending with the flour mixture. Mix until just combined. Do not overmix.
6. Bake:
    - Pour the batter into the prepared loaf pan and smooth the top with a spatula.
7. Bake in the preheated oven for 45-55 minutes, or until a toothpick inserted into the center comes out clean. If the top begins to brown too quickly, cover loosely with foil during baking.

8. Cool in Pan:
    - Allow the cake to cool in the pan for 10 minutes, then remove it from the pan and transfer it to a wire rack to cool completely.
9. Prepare Honey Glaze:
    - In a small bowl, whisk together the honey and hot water until smooth. Drizzle the glaze over the cooled cake.
10. Serve:
    - Slice and serve the Honey Ginger Tea Cake with a cup of tea or coffee. Enjoy the moist and flavorful cake with its delightful honey and ginger flavors!

This Honey Ginger Tea Cake is perfect for tea time or as a simple dessert. It's moist, fragrant, and infused with the wonderful combination of honey and ginger, making it a delightful treat for any occasion.

Honey Poached Pears

Ingredients:

- 4 ripe but firm pears (such as Bosc or Bartlett)
- 1 cup water
- 1/2 cup honey
- 1 cinnamon stick (optional)
- 1 teaspoon vanilla extract
- 1 strip of lemon peel (optional)
- Whipped cream, vanilla ice cream, or yogurt for serving (optional)
- Chopped nuts or mint leaves for garnish (optional)

Instructions:

1. Prepare the Pears:
    - Peel the pears, leaving the stems intact if desired. Slice a thin piece off the bottom of each pear so they can stand upright.
2. Poaching Liquid:
    - In a medium saucepan, combine the water, honey, cinnamon stick (if using), vanilla extract, and lemon peel (if using). Stir to combine.
3. Poach the Pears:
    - Place the saucepan over medium heat and bring the poaching liquid to a simmer.
    - Add the pears to the saucepan, standing them upright. The liquid should cover the pears at least halfway. If needed, add more water to cover.
4. Simmer:
    - Reduce the heat to low and simmer the pears gently, partially covered, for about 20-30 minutes, or until the pears are tender when pierced with a knife. The exact time will depend on the ripeness of your pears.
5. Cool:
    - Once tender, carefully remove the pears from the poaching liquid using a slotted spoon and transfer them to a plate or shallow bowl. Discard the cinnamon stick and lemon peel.
6. Reduce the Poaching Liquid (Optional):
    - Increase the heat to medium-high and simmer the poaching liquid until it reduces and thickens slightly, about 10-15 minutes. This will create a syrupy sauce.
7. Serve:
    - Serve the poached pears warm or chilled. Drizzle them with the reduced poaching liquid (if desired) and serve with whipped cream, vanilla ice cream, or yogurt.
    - Garnish with chopped nuts or mint leaves for added flavor and presentation.
8. Enjoy:
    - Enjoy your Honey Poached Pears as a delightful and elegant dessert!

This dessert is not only visually appealing but also showcases the natural sweetness of the pears enhanced by the honey and other aromatic flavors. It's perfect for entertaining or a special treat after a meal.

Honey Ricotta Cheesecake

Ingredients:

For the Crust:

- 1 1/2 cups graham cracker crumbs (about 12 whole graham crackers)
- 1/4 cup granulated sugar
- 1/2 cup unsalted butter, melted

For the Filling:

- 2 cups whole milk ricotta cheese
- 1 cup cream cheese, softened
- 3/4 cup honey
- 3 large eggs
- 1/4 cup all-purpose flour
- 1 teaspoon vanilla extract
- Zest of 1 lemon
- Pinch of salt

For the Honey Glaze (optional):

- 1/4 cup honey
- 1 tablespoon hot water

Instructions:

1. Preheat Oven:
   - Preheat your oven to 325°F (160°C). Grease a 9-inch springform pan and line the bottom with parchment paper.
2. Make the Crust:
   - In a medium bowl, combine the graham cracker crumbs, sugar, and melted butter. Mix until the crumbs are evenly moistened.
3. Press into Pan:
   - Press the crumb mixture firmly into the bottom of the prepared springform pan, forming an even layer. Use the back of a spoon or the bottom of a glass to compact the crumbs.
4. Make the Filling:
   - In a large bowl, beat together the ricotta cheese, cream cheese, and honey until smooth and creamy.
   - Add the eggs one at a time, beating well after each addition.
   - Stir in the flour, vanilla extract, lemon zest, and a pinch of salt until well combined.
5. Pour into Crust:

- Pour the filling over the prepared crust in the springform pan. Smooth the top with a spatula.
6. **Bake:**
    - Bake in the preheated oven for 55-65 minutes, or until the cheesecake is set around the edges but slightly jiggly in the center.
7. **Cool:**
    - Turn off the oven and let the cheesecake cool in the oven with the door slightly ajar for about 1 hour. This helps prevent cracking.
    - Remove the cheesecake from the oven and let it cool completely on a wire rack. Then refrigerate for at least 4 hours or overnight to chill and set.
8. **Prepare Honey Glaze (optional):**
    - In a small bowl, whisk together the honey and hot water until smooth. Drizzle the glaze over the cooled cheesecake before serving.
9. **Serve:**
    - Release the cheesecake from the springform pan and transfer it to a serving platter.
    - Slice and serve the Honey Ricotta Cheesecake chilled, optionally drizzling each slice with additional honey if desired.

This Honey Ricotta Cheesecake is creamy, subtly sweetened with honey, and has a delightful texture from the ricotta cheese. It's a perfect dessert for special occasions or any time you want to treat yourself to a luxurious dessert!

Honey Spice Cake

Ingredients:

For the Cake:

- 2 cups all-purpose flour
- 1 teaspoon baking powder
- 1/2 teaspoon baking soda
- 1/2 teaspoon salt
- 1 teaspoon ground cinnamon
- 1/2 teaspoon ground ginger
- 1/4 teaspoon ground cloves
- 1/4 teaspoon ground nutmeg
- 1/2 cup unsalted butter, softened
- 1/2 cup honey
- 1/2 cup granulated sugar
- 2 large eggs
- 1 teaspoon vanilla extract
- 1 cup buttermilk

For the Honey Glaze:

- 1/4 cup honey
- 1 tablespoon hot water

Instructions:

1. Preheat Oven and Prepare Pan:
    - Preheat your oven to 350°F (175°C). Grease and flour a 9-inch round cake pan or line it with parchment paper.
2. Mix Dry Ingredients:
    - In a medium bowl, whisk together the flour, baking powder, baking soda, salt, cinnamon, ginger, cloves, and nutmeg until well combined. Set aside.
3. Cream Butter, Honey, and Sugar:
    - In a large bowl, beat the softened butter, honey, and granulated sugar together until light and fluffy.
4. Add Eggs and Vanilla:
    - Beat in the eggs one at a time, mixing well after each addition. Stir in the vanilla extract.
5. Alternate Mixing:
    - Gradually add the dry ingredients to the butter mixture in three additions, alternating with the buttermilk, beginning and ending with the dry ingredients. Mix until just combined, being careful not to overmix.
6. Bake:

- Pour the batter into the prepared cake pan and smooth the top with a spatula.
7. Bake in the preheated oven for 30-35 minutes, or until a toothpick inserted into the center comes out clean.
8. Cool:
    - Allow the cake to cool in the pan for 10 minutes, then remove it from the pan and transfer it to a wire rack to cool completely.
9. Prepare Honey Glaze:
    - In a small bowl, whisk together the honey and hot water until smooth. Drizzle the glaze over the cooled cake.
10. Serve:
    - Slice and serve the Honey Spice Cake at room temperature. Enjoy the moist and flavorful cake with its delightful blend of spices and honey sweetness!

This Honey Spice Cake is perfect for afternoon tea, dessert, or any special occasion where you want to impress with a homemade treat. It's moist, fragrant, and full of warming spices that pair beautifully with the natural sweetness of honey.

Honey Vanilla Bean Madeleines

Ingredients:

- 2/3 cup all-purpose flour
- 1/2 teaspoon baking powder
- 1/4 teaspoon salt
- 2 large eggs, at room temperature
- 1/3 cup granulated sugar
- 2 tablespoons honey
- 1 teaspoon vanilla extract
- 1 vanilla bean pod, seeds scraped out (optional for extra vanilla flavor)
- 6 tablespoons unsalted butter, melted and cooled, plus extra for greasing the madeleine molds
- Powdered sugar, for dusting (optional)

Instructions:

1. Prepare the Madeleine Pans:
    - Brush the indentations of a madeleine mold with melted butter. Dust lightly with flour, tapping out any excess. Place the mold in the refrigerator or freezer while you prepare the batter.
2. Mix Dry Ingredients:
    - In a small bowl, whisk together the flour, baking powder, and salt. Set aside.
3. Whisk Eggs and Sugar:
    - In a large bowl, whisk together the eggs, granulated sugar, honey, vanilla extract, and scraped vanilla bean seeds (if using) until pale and fluffy, about 5 minutes with a hand mixer or 3 minutes with a stand mixer.
4. Fold in Dry Ingredients:
    - Gently fold the dry ingredients into the egg mixture using a spatula, taking care not to deflate the batter.
5. Add Melted Butter:
    - Pour the melted butter into the batter and fold gently until fully incorporated.
6. Chill the Batter:
    - Cover the bowl with plastic wrap and refrigerate for at least 1 hour, or up to 12 hours. Chilling the batter helps ensure the characteristic hump on the madeleines.
7. Preheat Oven:
    - Preheat your oven to 375°F (190°C) and position a rack in the center of the oven.
8. Fill the Madeleine Molds:
    - Spoon 1 tablespoon of batter into each prepared madeleine mold, filling each about 3/4 full.
9. Bake:
    - Bake for 10-12 minutes, or until the edges are golden brown and the centers are puffed up.

10. Cool and Serve:
    - Remove the madeleines from the oven and immediately tap the mold against a flat surface to release them. Transfer the madeleines to a wire rack to cool completely.
11. Dust with Powdered Sugar (Optional):
    - Dust the cooled madeleines with powdered sugar before serving, if desired.
12. Enjoy:
    - Serve the Honey Vanilla Bean Madeleines with tea or coffee, or as a delightful dessert. They are best enjoyed fresh on the day they are made.

These Honey Vanilla Bean Madeleines are a treat with their delicate crumb and subtle sweetness from the honey and vanilla. They make a lovely addition to any tea party or special occasion. Enjoy baking and savoring these delightful French treats!

Honey Date Bars

Ingredients:

For the Date Filling:

- 2 cups pitted dates, chopped
- 1/2 cup water
- 1 tablespoon lemon juice
- 1/2 teaspoon vanilla extract
- Pinch of salt

For the Oatmeal Crust:

- 1 1/2 cups old-fashioned rolled oats
- 1 cup all-purpose flour
- 1/2 cup brown sugar, packed
- 1/2 teaspoon baking soda
- 1/4 teaspoon salt
- 1/2 cup unsalted butter, melted
- 1/4 cup honey
- 1 teaspoon vanilla extract

Instructions:

1. Prepare the Date Filling:
    - In a medium saucepan, combine the chopped dates, water, lemon juice, vanilla extract, and a pinch of salt.
    - Bring the mixture to a simmer over medium heat. Cook, stirring occasionally, for about 5-7 minutes, or until the dates are soft and the mixture has thickened into a paste-like consistency.
    - Remove from heat and let the date filling cool slightly.
2. Preheat Oven and Prepare Pan:
    - Preheat your oven to 350°F (175°C). Grease an 8x8 inch baking pan or line it with parchment paper, leaving an overhang for easy removal.
3. Make the Oatmeal Crust:
    - In a large bowl, combine the rolled oats, all-purpose flour, brown sugar, baking soda, and salt.
    - Stir in the melted butter, honey, and vanilla extract until the mixture resembles coarse crumbs and is well combined.
4. Assemble the Bars:
    - Press half of the oatmeal crust mixture firmly into the bottom of the prepared baking pan, creating an even layer.
    - Spread the cooled date filling evenly over the crust layer, using a spatula to smooth it out.

5. Add the Top Crust:
     - Sprinkle the remaining oatmeal crust mixture evenly over the date filling, pressing down lightly with your hands or the back of a spoon.
6. Bake:
     - Bake in the preheated oven for 25-30 minutes, or until the top is golden brown.
7. Cool and Slice:
     - Remove from the oven and let the Honey Date Bars cool completely in the pan on a wire rack.
     - Once cooled, lift the bars out of the pan using the parchment paper overhang and transfer them to a cutting board. Cut into squares or bars.
8. Serve:
     - Enjoy the Honey Date Bars as a wholesome snack or dessert. Store any leftovers in an airtight container at room temperature for up to 5 days.

These Honey Date Bars are chewy, sweet, and satisfying, making them perfect for breakfast on-the-go or as a midday pick-me-up. The natural sweetness of honey and dates pairs beautifully with the hearty oatmeal crust.

Honey Pumpkin Pie

Ingredients:

For the Pie Crust:

- 1 1/4 cups all-purpose flour
- 1/2 teaspoon salt
- 1/2 teaspoon granulated sugar
- 1/2 cup unsalted butter, cold and cut into small pieces
- 2-4 tablespoons ice water

For the Filling:

- 1 can (15 ounces) pumpkin puree (not pumpkin pie filling)
- 3/4 cup honey
- 1/2 cup heavy cream
- 1/2 cup milk
- 2 large eggs
- 1 teaspoon vanilla extract
- 1 teaspoon ground cinnamon
- 1/2 teaspoon ground ginger
- 1/4 teaspoon ground nutmeg
- 1/4 teaspoon ground cloves
- 1/4 teaspoon salt

Instructions:

1. Prepare the Pie Crust:
    - In a large bowl, whisk together the flour, salt, and sugar.
    - Add the cold butter pieces and cut in using a pastry blender or fork until the mixture resembles coarse crumbs.
    - Gradually add the ice water, 1 tablespoon at a time, and mix with a fork until the dough begins to come together.
    - Gather the dough into a ball, flatten into a disk, wrap in plastic wrap, and refrigerate for at least 1 hour.
2. Preheat Oven:
    - Preheat your oven to 375°F (190°C).
3. Roll out the Pie Crust:
    - On a lightly floured surface, roll out the chilled dough into a circle about 12 inches in diameter. Carefully transfer the dough to a 9-inch pie dish. Trim and crimp the edges as desired.
4. Make the Filling:

- In a large bowl, whisk together the pumpkin puree, honey, heavy cream, milk, eggs, vanilla extract, spices (cinnamon, ginger, nutmeg, cloves), and salt until smooth and well combined.
5. Pour the Filling into the Pie Crust:
   - Pour the pumpkin filling into the prepared pie crust, spreading it evenly.
6. Bake the Pie:
   - Place the pie in the preheated oven and bake for 45-50 minutes, or until the filling is set and the center is slightly jiggly.
7. Cool and Serve:
   - Remove the pie from the oven and let it cool completely on a wire rack.
   - Once cooled, refrigerate the pie for at least 2 hours or overnight to allow the flavors to develop.
8. Serve:
   - Serve slices of Honey Pumpkin Pie chilled or at room temperature. Optionally, top with whipped cream before serving.

This Honey Pumpkin Pie is creamy, flavorful, and subtly sweetened with honey, making it a perfect dessert for Thanksgiving or any fall gathering. Enjoy the warm spices and rich pumpkin flavor in every bite!

Honey Almond Biscotti

Ingredients:

- 2 cups all-purpose flour
- 1 teaspoon baking powder
- 1/4 teaspoon salt
- 1/2 cup unsalted butter, softened
- 1/2 cup granulated sugar
- 1/4 cup honey
- 2 large eggs
- 1 teaspoon vanilla extract
- 1/2 cup almonds, coarsely chopped (or slivered)
- 1/2 cup almond meal (ground almonds)

Optional:

- 1/2 cup dark chocolate, melted (for dipping)

Instructions:

1. Preheat Oven and Prepare Baking Sheet:
    - Preheat your oven to 350°F (175°C). Line a baking sheet with parchment paper.
2. Mix Dry Ingredients:
    - In a medium bowl, whisk together the flour, baking powder, and salt. Stir in the almond meal (ground almonds) until well combined. Set aside.
3. Cream Butter, Sugar, and Honey:
    - In a large bowl, cream together the softened butter, granulated sugar, and honey until light and fluffy.
4. Add Eggs and Vanilla:
    - Beat in the eggs, one at a time, until well combined. Stir in the vanilla extract.
5. Combine Wet and Dry Ingredients:
    - Gradually add the dry ingredients to the wet mixture, mixing until just combined. Fold in the chopped almonds until evenly distributed in the dough.
6. Shape the Dough:
    - Divide the dough in half. On a lightly floured surface, shape each half into a log about 12 inches long and 2 inches wide. Place the logs on the prepared baking sheet, spacing them a few inches apart.
7. Bake First Bake:
    - Bake in the preheated oven for 25-30 minutes, or until the logs are firm to the touch and lightly golden brown. Remove from the oven and let cool on the baking sheet for 15 minutes. Keep the oven on.
8. Slice the Biscotti:
    - Using a serrated knife, carefully slice the logs diagonally into 1/2-inch thick slices. Place the slices cut side down on the baking sheet.

9. **Second Bake:**
   - Bake the biscotti for an additional 10-12 minutes, turning them over halfway through baking, until they are golden and crisp. Remove from the oven and let cool completely on a wire rack.
10. **Optional: Dip in Chocolate (if desired):**
    - Melt the dark chocolate in a microwave-safe bowl in 30-second intervals, stirring in between, until smooth. Dip one end of each cooled biscotti into the melted chocolate and place on parchment paper to set.
11. **Serve and Store:**
    - Once the chocolate has set (if using), serve the Honey Almond Biscotti with coffee, tea, or as a delightful snack. Store in an airtight container at room temperature for up to 2 weeks.

These Honey Almond Biscotti are crunchy, nutty, and subtly sweetened with honey, making them a perfect treat for any occasion. Enjoy the combination of almonds and honey in this classic Italian cookie!

Honey Apple Crisp

Ingredients:

For the Apple Filling:

- 6 cups apples, peeled, cored, and thinly sliced (about 5-6 medium apples, such as Granny Smith or Honeycrisp)
- 1/4 cup honey
- 1 tablespoon lemon juice
- 1 teaspoon ground cinnamon
- 1/4 teaspoon ground nutmeg
- 1/4 teaspoon salt

For the Crisp Topping:

- 1 cup old-fashioned rolled oats
- 1/2 cup all-purpose flour
- 1/2 cup packed brown sugar
- 1/4 teaspoon salt
- 1/2 cup unsalted butter, cold and cut into small pieces
- 1/4 cup honey
- 1/2 cup chopped nuts (such as pecans or walnuts) - optional for added crunch

Instructions:

1. Preheat Oven:
    - Preheat your oven to 350°F (175°C). Lightly grease a 9x9 inch baking dish or a similar size baking dish.
2. Prepare the Apple Filling:
    - In a large bowl, combine the sliced apples, honey, lemon juice, cinnamon, nutmeg, and salt. Toss together until the apples are evenly coated with the honey and spices.
3. Transfer to Baking Dish:
    - Spread the apple mixture evenly in the prepared baking dish.
4. Make the Crisp Topping:
    - In a medium bowl, combine the rolled oats, flour, brown sugar, and salt.
    - Cut in the cold butter using a pastry blender or fork until the mixture resembles coarse crumbs.
    - Stir in the honey and chopped nuts (if using) until the mixture is evenly combined.
5. Assemble and Bake:
    - Sprinkle the crisp topping evenly over the apple filling in the baking dish, covering it completely.
6. Bake in Preheated Oven:

- Bake for 35-40 minutes, or until the topping is golden brown and the apple filling is bubbly around the edges.
7. Cool and Serve:
    - Remove from the oven and let the Honey Apple Crisp cool slightly before serving. Serve warm with a scoop of vanilla ice cream or a dollop of whipped cream, if desired.
8. Enjoy:
    - Enjoy this comforting Honey Apple Crisp as a delicious dessert, perfect for cool evenings or as a treat for family and friends.

This Honey Apple Crisp combines the natural sweetness of honey with the tartness of apples, enhanced by warm spices and a crunchy oat topping. It's a classic dessert that's sure to be a hit!

Honey Lemon Meringue Pie

Ingredients:

For the Pie Crust:

- 1 1/4 cups all-purpose flour
- 1/2 teaspoon salt
- 1/2 teaspoon granulated sugar
- 1/2 cup unsalted butter, cold and cut into small pieces
- 2-4 tablespoons ice water

For the Lemon Filling:

- 1 cup granulated sugar
- 1/4 cup cornstarch
- 1/4 teaspoon salt
- 1 1/2 cups water
- 4 large egg yolks, beaten
- 1 tablespoon lemon zest
- 1/2 cup fresh lemon juice (about 3-4 lemons)
- 1/4 cup honey
- 2 tablespoons unsalted butter

For the Meringue Topping:

- 4 large egg whites, at room temperature
- 1/4 teaspoon cream of tartar
- 1/2 cup granulated sugar
- 1/2 teaspoon vanilla extract

Instructions:

1. Make the Pie Crust:
    - In a large bowl, whisk together the flour, salt, and sugar. Add the cold butter pieces and use a pastry blender or fork to cut the butter into the flour mixture until it resembles coarse crumbs.
    - Gradually add the ice water, 1 tablespoon at a time, mixing with a fork until the dough begins to come together. Gather the dough into a ball, flatten into a disk, wrap in plastic wrap, and refrigerate for at least 1 hour.
2. Prepare the Pie Crust:
    - Preheat your oven to 375°F (190°C). On a lightly floured surface, roll out the chilled dough into a circle about 12 inches in diameter. Carefully transfer the dough to a 9-inch pie dish. Trim and crimp the edges as desired. Prick the bottom and sides of the crust with a fork.
3. Blind Bake the Crust:

- Line the chilled pie crust with parchment paper or aluminum foil, and fill with pie weights or dried beans. Bake in the preheated oven for 15 minutes. Remove the weights and parchment/foil, and bake for an additional 10-12 minutes, or until the crust is golden brown. Remove from oven and let cool completely on a wire rack.
4. Make the Lemon Filling:
    - In a medium saucepan, whisk together the sugar, cornstarch, and salt. Gradually whisk in the water until smooth. Cook over medium heat, stirring constantly, until the mixture thickens and comes to a boil.
    - Boil for 1 minute, then remove from heat. Gradually whisk about 1/2 cup of the hot mixture into the beaten egg yolks to temper them. Gradually whisk the tempered egg yolks back into the saucepan mixture.
    - Return the saucepan to the heat and bring to a gentle boil, stirring constantly, for 2 minutes. Remove from heat and stir in the lemon zest, lemon juice, honey, and butter until smooth. Pour the lemon filling into the cooled pie crust.
5. Make the Meringue Topping:
    - In a clean, dry bowl, beat the egg whites and cream of tartar with a hand mixer or stand mixer fitted with the whisk attachment until soft peaks form.
    - Gradually add the granulated sugar, 1 tablespoon at a time, while continuing to beat on high speed until stiff, glossy peaks form. Beat in the vanilla extract.
6. Top the Pie with Meringue:
    - Spread the meringue evenly over the hot lemon filling, making sure to spread it all the way to the edges of the crust to seal it.
7. Bake the Pie:
    - Bake the pie in the preheated oven at 350°F (175°C) for 12-15 minutes, or until the meringue is lightly golden brown.
8. Cool and Serve:
    - Remove from the oven and let the pie cool completely on a wire rack. Chill in the refrigerator for at least 3 hours before serving to set the filling.
9. Slice and Enjoy:
    - Slice the Honey Lemon Meringue Pie and serve chilled. Enjoy the sweet-tart flavor combination with a fluffy meringue topping!

This Honey Lemon Meringue Pie is sure to be a hit with its tangy lemon filling enhanced by the natural sweetness of honey, all topped with a light and fluffy meringue. It's a perfect dessert for special occasions or any time you crave a delightful treat!

Honey Rosewater Ice Cream

Ingredients:

- 2 cups heavy cream
- 1 cup whole milk
- 3/4 cup honey
- 4 large egg yolks
- 1 teaspoon rosewater
- 1/4 teaspoon salt
- Optional: Dried rose petals for garnish

Instructions:

1. Prepare the Ice Cream Base:
    - In a saucepan, combine the heavy cream, whole milk, and honey over medium heat. Stir occasionally until the mixture is steaming and just begins to simmer. Do not let it boil.
2. Temper the Egg Yolks:
    - In a separate bowl, whisk the egg yolks until smooth. Gradually whisk in about 1/2 cup of the warm cream mixture into the yolks to temper them, whisking constantly to prevent curdling.
3. Combine and Cook:
    - Pour the tempered egg yolk mixture back into the saucepan with the remaining cream mixture. Cook over medium heat, stirring constantly with a wooden spoon or heatproof spatula, until the mixture thickens slightly and coats the back of the spoon, about 5-7 minutes. Do not let it boil.
4. Strain the Custard:
    - Remove the custard from heat and immediately strain it through a fine-mesh sieve into a clean bowl to remove any lumps and ensure a smooth texture.
5. Add Flavorings:
    - Stir in the rosewater and salt until well combined. Adjust the amount of rosewater to your taste, as it can vary in potency.
6. Chill the Mixture:
    - Cover the bowl with plastic wrap, pressing it directly onto the surface of the custard to prevent a skin from forming. Refrigerate the mixture until completely chilled, at least 4 hours or overnight.
7. Churn the Ice Cream:
    - Once chilled, churn the custard in an ice cream maker according to the manufacturer's instructions until it reaches a soft-serve consistency.
8. Transfer and Freeze:
    - Transfer the churned ice cream to an airtight container. If desired, sprinkle dried rose petals on top for garnish. Press a piece of parchment paper or plastic wrap directly onto the surface of the ice cream to prevent ice crystals from forming. Cover tightly with the lid.

9. Final Freeze:
    - Freeze the ice cream for at least 4 hours or overnight until firm.
10. Serve:
    - Serve the Honey Rosewater Ice Cream scooped into bowls or cones. Enjoy the delicate floral notes and sweetness of honey in every creamy bite!

This Honey Rosewater Ice Cream is a refreshing and elegant dessert that pairs well with fresh berries or a drizzle of honey for added sweetness. It's perfect for special occasions or whenever you want to indulge in a unique and sophisticated treat.

Honey Cardamom Rice Pudding

Ingredients:

- 1/2 cup long-grain white rice (such as basmati)
- 4 cups whole milk
- 1/4 teaspoon salt
- 1/4 cup honey (adjust to taste)
- 1 teaspoon ground cardamom (or 4-5 whole cardamom pods, crushed)
- 1/2 teaspoon vanilla extract
- Optional toppings: Chopped nuts (like pistachios or almonds), dried fruits (such as raisins or chopped apricots), ground cinnamon for garnish

Instructions:

1. Cook the Rice:
    - Rinse the rice under cold water until the water runs clear. Drain well.
    - In a medium saucepan, combine the rinsed rice, milk, and salt. Bring to a boil over medium-high heat, stirring occasionally to prevent the rice from sticking to the bottom of the pan.
2. Simmer the Rice:
    - Once boiling, reduce the heat to low and simmer uncovered, stirring frequently, for about 20-25 minutes or until the rice is tender and the mixture has thickened to a pudding-like consistency.
3. Add Honey and Cardamom:
    - Stir in the honey, ground cardamom (or crushed cardamom pods), and vanilla extract. Continue to cook over low heat for an additional 5-10 minutes, stirring occasionally, to allow the flavors to meld together.
4. Adjust Sweetness:
    - Taste and adjust the sweetness by adding more honey if desired. Remember that the sweetness will slightly mellow once the pudding cools.
5. Serve:
    - Remove the rice pudding from heat. Remove the crushed cardamom pods if using whole pods. Serve warm or chilled, garnished with chopped nuts, dried fruits, and a sprinkle of ground cinnamon if desired.
6. Chill (Optional):
    - If serving chilled, transfer the rice pudding to individual serving dishes or a large bowl. Cover with plastic wrap pressed directly onto the surface of the pudding to prevent a skin from forming. Chill in the refrigerator for at least 2 hours or until ready to serve.
7. Enjoy:
    - Serve the Honey Cardamom Rice Pudding as a comforting dessert or snack. It's delicious either warm or chilled, with the aromatic flavors of cardamom and the sweetness of honey complementing each other perfectly.

This Honey Cardamom Rice Pudding recipe is versatile and can be customized with your favorite toppings or additional spices to suit your taste preferences. It's a wonderful dessert that brings warmth and comfort with every spoonful!

Honey Fig Jam

Ingredients:

- 1 pound fresh figs, stems removed and quartered
- 3/4 cup honey
- 1/4 cup water
- 1 tablespoon lemon juice
- 1/2 teaspoon lemon zest
- 1/4 teaspoon ground cinnamon (optional)

Instructions:

1. Prepare the Figs:
   - Wash the figs thoroughly under cold water. Remove the stems and quarter the figs.
2. Cook the Jam:
   - In a medium saucepan, combine the quartered figs, honey, water, lemon juice, lemon zest, and ground cinnamon (if using). Stir well to combine.
3. Simmer the Mixture:
   - Bring the mixture to a boil over medium-high heat, stirring occasionally. Once boiling, reduce the heat to low and let it simmer uncovered for about 30-40 minutes, or until the figs have softened and the mixture has thickened to a jam-like consistency. Stir occasionally to prevent sticking.
4. Mash or Blend (Optional):
   - For a smoother consistency, use a potato masher or immersion blender to break down some of the fig pieces. This step is optional depending on your preference for texture.
5. Test for Doneness:
   - To test if the jam is ready, place a small amount on a chilled plate. If it thickens and holds its shape without running, it is done.
6. Cool and Store:
   - Remove the saucepan from heat and let the jam cool to room temperature. Transfer the jam to clean, sterilized jars with tight-fitting lids.
7. Store the Jam:
   - Seal the jars tightly and store the Honey Fig Jam in the refrigerator for up to 3 weeks. For longer storage, you can also process the jars in a hot water bath for 10-15 minutes to seal them properly and store in a cool, dark place.
8. Enjoy:
   - Serve the Honey Fig Jam on toast, crackers, or as a topping for yogurt or cheese. It also makes a wonderful filling for pastries or as a sweet addition to meat and cheese platters.

This homemade Honey Fig Jam captures the delicious sweetness of figs enhanced by the natural honey flavor, perfect for enjoying year-round or gifting to friends and family.

Honey Plum Galette

Ingredients:

For the Galette Dough:

- 1 1/4 cups all-purpose flour
- 1/2 teaspoon salt
- 1 tablespoon granulated sugar
- 1/2 cup unsalted butter, cold and cut into small pieces
- 2-4 tablespoons ice water

For the Filling:

- 4-5 ripe plums, pitted and sliced (about 2 cups sliced)
- 2 tablespoons honey
- 1 tablespoon cornstarch
- 1/2 teaspoon ground cinnamon
- 1/4 teaspoon ground nutmeg
- Zest of 1 lemon
- 1 tablespoon lemon juice

For Assembly:

- 1 egg, beaten (for egg wash)
- 1 tablespoon coarse sugar (such as turbinado or demerara) for sprinkling
- Optional: Vanilla ice cream or whipped cream for serving

Instructions:

1. Prepare the Galette Dough:
    - In a large bowl, whisk together the flour, salt, and sugar. Add the cold butter pieces and use a pastry blender or fork to cut the butter into the flour mixture until it resembles coarse crumbs.
    - Gradually add the ice water, 1 tablespoon at a time, mixing with a fork until the dough begins to come together. Gather the dough into a ball, flatten into a disk, wrap in plastic wrap, and refrigerate for at least 1 hour.
2. Preheat Oven:
    - Preheat your oven to 375°F (190°C). Line a baking sheet with parchment paper.
3. Prepare the Filling:
    - In a medium bowl, combine the sliced plums, honey, cornstarch, ground cinnamon, ground nutmeg, lemon zest, and lemon juice. Toss gently to coat the plums evenly with the honey and spices. Set aside.
4. Roll out the Dough:

- On a lightly floured surface, roll out the chilled dough into a circle about 12 inches in diameter and 1/8 inch thick. Transfer the rolled dough to the prepared baking sheet.
5. Assemble the Galette:
    - Arrange the plum slices in the center of the rolled-out dough, leaving about a 2-inch border around the edges. Fold the edges of the dough over the filling, pleating as you go and leaving the center of the galette exposed.
6. Brush with Egg Wash:
    - Brush the edges of the dough with the beaten egg. This will help create a golden crust when baked.
7. Sprinkle with Sugar:
    - Sprinkle the coarse sugar over the exposed plum slices and the edges of the galette.
8. Bake the Galette:
    - Bake in the preheated oven for 35-40 minutes, or until the crust is golden brown and the plum filling is bubbling.
9. Cool and Serve:
    - Remove from the oven and let the Honey Plum Galette cool slightly on the baking sheet. Transfer to a wire rack to cool completely before slicing.
10. Serve:
    - Serve slices of the Honey Plum Galette warm or at room temperature. Optionally, serve with a scoop of vanilla ice cream or a dollop of whipped cream for an extra indulgent treat.

This Honey Plum Galette is a rustic and elegant dessert that highlights the natural sweetness of plums enhanced by honey and warming spices, all wrapped in a flaky, buttery crust. Enjoy this delicious galette as a perfect ending to any meal!

Honey Cranberry Sauce (as a sweet condiment)

Ingredients:

- 12 ounces fresh cranberries
- 1/2 cup honey
- 1/2 cup orange juice (freshly squeezed)
- Zest of 1 orange (optional)
- 1/4 teaspoon ground cinnamon (optional)
- Pinch of salt

Instructions:

1. Combine Ingredients:
    - In a medium saucepan, combine the cranberries, honey, orange juice, orange zest (if using), ground cinnamon (if using), and a pinch of salt.
2. Cook Over Medium Heat:
    - Bring the mixture to a boil over medium-high heat, stirring occasionally.
3. Simmer:
    - Once boiling, reduce the heat to medium-low and let the mixture simmer for about 10-15 minutes, or until the cranberries burst and the sauce thickens to your desired consistency. Stir occasionally to prevent sticking.
4. Adjust Sweetness:
    - Taste the cranberry sauce and adjust the sweetness by adding more honey if desired. Keep in mind that the sauce will thicken slightly as it cools.
5. Cool and Serve:
    - Remove the saucepan from heat and let the Honey Cranberry Sauce cool to room temperature. Transfer to a serving bowl or an airtight container.
6. Chill (Optional):
    - If you prefer a chilled cranberry sauce, cover the bowl or container with plastic wrap pressed directly onto the surface of the sauce to prevent a skin from forming. Chill in the refrigerator for at least 2 hours or until ready to serve.
7. Serve:
    - Serve the Honey Cranberry Sauce alongside roast turkey, chicken, pork, or as a condiment for sandwiches. It also pairs well with cheese boards or as a topping for desserts like cheesecake or yogurt.

This Honey Cranberry Sauce adds a delightful sweetness and citrusy flavor to traditional cranberry sauce, making it a versatile and tasty addition to your holiday or everyday meals. Enjoy the burst of flavors in every spoonful!

Honey Cherry Clafoutis

Ingredients:

- 1 cup fresh cherries, pitted (about 12 ounces)
- 3 large eggs
- 1/2 cup all-purpose flour
- 1/2 cup honey
- 1 cup whole milk
- 1 teaspoon vanilla extract
- Pinch of salt
- Powdered sugar, for dusting (optional)
- Butter or cooking spray, for greasing the baking dish

Instructions:

1. Preheat Oven:
    - Preheat your oven to 350°F (175°C). Grease a 9-inch pie dish or baking dish with butter or cooking spray.
2. Prepare Cherries:
    - Wash and pit the cherries. If using sweet cherries, you can halve them. Sour cherries are traditionally used in clafoutis, but both work well.
3. Make Batter:
    - In a large bowl, whisk together the eggs, flour, honey, milk, vanilla extract, and salt until smooth and well combined. The batter will be thin, similar to pancake batter.
4. Assemble Clafoutis:
    - Arrange the pitted cherries evenly in the greased baking dish.
5. Pour Batter Over Cherries:
    - Pour the batter over the cherries in the baking dish. The cherries may float to the top, which is normal.
6. Bake:
    - Bake in the preheated oven for 35-40 minutes, or until the clafoutis is puffed and golden brown on top, and a toothpick inserted into the center comes out clean.
7. Cool:
    - Remove from the oven and let the Honey Cherry Clafoutis cool slightly. It will deflate a bit as it cools.
8. Serve:
    - Dust with powdered sugar if desired. Serve the clafoutis warm or at room temperature, either on its own or with a dollop of whipped cream or a scoop of vanilla ice cream.
9. Enjoy:
    - Enjoy this Honey Cherry Clafoutis as a delicious and elegant dessert, highlighting the natural sweetness of cherries combined with the subtle flavor of honey in every bite.

Clafoutis is best served fresh on the day it's made, but leftovers can be refrigerated and enjoyed chilled or gently reheated in the oven. It's a versatile dessert that works well for both casual meals and special occasions.

Honey Sesame Brittle

Ingredients:

- 1 cup granulated sugar
- 1/2 cup honey
- 1/4 cup water
- 1/4 teaspoon salt
- 1 cup sesame seeds
- 1 tablespoon unsalted butter
- 1 teaspoon vanilla extract
- 1/2 teaspoon baking soda

Instructions:

1. Prepare Baking Sheet:
    - Line a large baking sheet with parchment paper or a silicone baking mat. Lightly grease the parchment paper with butter or cooking spray.
2. Toast Sesame Seeds:
    - In a dry skillet over medium heat, toast the sesame seeds until they are lightly golden and fragrant, stirring frequently. Be careful not to burn them. Remove from heat and set aside.
3. Prepare Brittle Mixture:
    - In a medium saucepan, combine the granulated sugar, honey, water, and salt. Cook over medium-high heat, stirring constantly until the sugar dissolves.
4. Cook to Soft Ball Stage:
    - Insert a candy thermometer into the mixture and continue to cook, without stirring, until the temperature reaches 300°F (150°C), which is the hard crack stage. This should take about 10-15 minutes.
5. Add Sesame Seeds and Butter:
    - Once at the desired temperature, immediately remove from heat and stir in the toasted sesame seeds, butter, and vanilla extract. Be cautious as the mixture will bubble up when these ingredients are added.
6. Add Baking Soda:
    - Quickly stir in the baking soda until well combined. The mixture will foam and lighten in color.
7. Pour and Spread:
    - Pour the hot brittle mixture onto the prepared baking sheet. Use a heatproof spatula or spoon to spread it out evenly into a thin layer. Work quickly as the mixture will begin to set fast.
8. Cool and Break:
    - Let the brittle cool completely at room temperature until hardened and cooled. Once cooled, break the brittle into pieces using your hands or a knife.
9. Store:

- Store the Honey Sesame Brittle in an airtight container at room temperature for up to 2 weeks. Separate layers with parchment paper to prevent sticking.

10. Enjoy:
    - Enjoy the Honey Sesame Brittle as a crunchy snack or a sweet topping for desserts like ice cream or yogurt. It's a delightful treat with a perfect balance of sweetness and nuttiness!

This Honey Sesame Brittle recipe provides a satisfying crunch and a deliciously sweet flavor, making it a wonderful homemade snack or gift idea for any occasion.

Honey Banana Popsicles

Ingredients:

- 2 ripe bananas
- 1 cup plain yogurt (Greek yogurt or regular yogurt)
- 2-3 tablespoons honey (adjust to taste)
- 1 teaspoon vanilla extract (optional)

Instructions:

1. Prepare Ingredients:
   - Peel the bananas and cut them into chunks.
2. Blend Ingredients:
   - In a blender or food processor, combine the banana chunks, yogurt, honey, and vanilla extract (if using). Blend until smooth and creamy.
3. Taste and Adjust:
   - Taste the mixture and adjust sweetness by adding more honey if desired.
4. Pour into Popsicle Molds:
   - Pour the blended mixture into popsicle molds, leaving a little space at the top for expansion. If you don't have molds, you can use small paper cups or ice cube trays with popsicle sticks inserted.
5. Freeze:
   - Insert popsicle sticks into the molds. Freeze the popsicles for at least 4 hours, or until completely frozen.
6. Unmold and Serve:
   - To unmold the popsicles, briefly run warm water over the outside of the molds to loosen them. Gently pull the popsicles out.
7. Enjoy:
   - Serve and enjoy these refreshing Honey Banana Popsicles as a healthy snack or dessert. They're perfect for kids and adults alike!

Variations:

- Chocolate Drizzle: Melt some dark chocolate and drizzle it over the frozen popsicles for a decadent touch.
- Nutty Crunch: Roll the frozen popsicles in chopped nuts (like almonds or peanuts) for added texture.
- Berry Twist: Add fresh or frozen berries (such as strawberries or blueberries) to the blender for a fruity twist.

These Honey Banana Popsicles are not only delicious but also customizable to suit your taste preferences. They are a great way to use up ripe bananas and enjoy a cool, nutritious treat at the same time!

Honey Pear Bread Pudding

Ingredients:

- 4 cups stale bread cubes (about 1-inch cubes, use French bread or any sturdy bread)
- 2 ripe pears, peeled, cored, and diced
- 4 large eggs
- 1 cup milk (whole milk or any milk of your choice)
- 1/2 cup heavy cream
- 1/2 cup honey
- 1 teaspoon vanilla extract
- 1/2 teaspoon ground cinnamon
- 1/4 teaspoon ground nutmeg
- Pinch of salt
- Butter, for greasing the baking dish
- Powdered sugar, for dusting (optional)

Instructions:

1. Preheat Oven:
    - Preheat your oven to 350°F (175°C). Grease a 9x9 inch baking dish with butter.
2. Prepare Bread and Pears:
    - Cut the stale bread into 1-inch cubes and place them in the greased baking dish. Dice the peeled and cored pears, and distribute them evenly over the bread cubes.
3. Make Custard Mixture:
    - In a large bowl, whisk together the eggs, milk, heavy cream, honey, vanilla extract, ground cinnamon, ground nutmeg, and a pinch of salt until well combined.
4. Pour Over Bread and Pears:
    - Pour the custard mixture evenly over the bread cubes and pears in the baking dish. Press down lightly on the bread cubes to ensure they are soaked in the custard.
5. Bake:
    - Place the baking dish in the preheated oven and bake for 35-40 minutes, or until the top is golden brown and the custard is set. The bread pudding should be puffed and slightly firm to the touch.
6. Cool and Serve:
    - Remove from the oven and let the Honey Pear Bread Pudding cool slightly before serving. Optionally, dust with powdered sugar before serving for a decorative touch.
7. Enjoy:
    - Serve warm or at room temperature. This Honey Pear Bread Pudding is delicious on its own, or you can serve it with a dollop of whipped cream, a drizzle of honey, or a scoop of vanilla ice cream for an extra treat.

This recipe for Honey Pear Bread Pudding is perfect for showcasing the sweetness of pears combined with the rich flavors of honey and spices. It's a comforting dessert that's great for any occasion, whether for a cozy family dinner or a special holiday gathering.

Honey Blueberry Pancakes

Ingredients:

- 1 cup all-purpose flour
- 1 tablespoon baking powder
- 1/4 teaspoon salt
- 1 tablespoon honey
- 1 cup milk (whole milk or buttermilk)
- 1 large egg
- 2 tablespoons unsalted butter, melted
- 1 teaspoon vanilla extract
- 1 cup fresh or frozen blueberries (if using frozen, do not thaw)

Instructions:

1. Prepare Dry Ingredients:
    - In a large bowl, whisk together the flour, baking powder, and salt.
2. Prepare Wet Ingredients:
    - In another bowl, whisk together the honey, milk, egg, melted butter, and vanilla extract until well combined.
3. Combine Wet and Dry Ingredients:
    - Pour the wet ingredients into the bowl with the dry ingredients. Stir gently with a spatula or wooden spoon until just combined. Do not overmix; a few lumps in the batter are okay.
4. Fold in Blueberries:
    - Gently fold the blueberries into the pancake batter. Be careful not to break the berries.
5. Heat the Griddle or Pan:
    - Heat a non-stick griddle or large skillet over medium heat. Lightly grease with butter or cooking spray.
6. Cook Pancakes:
    - Pour about 1/4 cup of batter onto the griddle for each pancake. Cook until bubbles form on the surface of the pancake and the edges look set, about 2-3 minutes.
7. Flip and Cook:
    - Carefully flip the pancakes with a spatula and cook for another 1-2 minutes, or until golden brown and cooked through.
8. Keep Warm:
    - Transfer the cooked pancakes to a plate and cover loosely with aluminum foil to keep warm while you cook the remaining pancakes.
9. Serve:
    - Serve the Honey Blueberry Pancakes warm, topped with additional blueberries, a drizzle of honey, and a pat of butter if desired.
10. Enjoy:

- Enjoy these fluffy and flavorful pancakes as a delicious breakfast or brunch treat!

These Honey Blueberry Pancakes are not only delicious but also customizable. You can substitute the blueberries with other berries or add nuts for extra texture. They're sure to become a favorite at your breakfast table!

Honey Raspberry Fool

Ingredients:

- 2 cups fresh raspberries (or frozen, thawed)
- 1/4 cup honey (adjust to taste)
- 1 tablespoon lemon juice
- 1 cup heavy cream
- 1/2 teaspoon vanilla extract
- Fresh raspberries and mint leaves, for garnish (optional)

Instructions:

1. Prepare the Raspberry Puree:
    - In a blender or food processor, puree the raspberries until smooth. Strain the puree through a fine-mesh sieve to remove the seeds, if desired.
2. Sweeten the Puree:
    - Transfer the raspberry puree to a bowl and stir in the honey and lemon juice. Adjust the sweetness to your taste preference.
3. Whip the Cream:
    - In a separate bowl, whip the heavy cream and vanilla extract until stiff peaks form.
4. Fold Raspberry Puree into Whipped Cream:
    - Gently fold the raspberry puree into the whipped cream until evenly combined. Be careful not to deflate the whipped cream too much.
5. Chill:
    - Cover the bowl with plastic wrap and chill the Honey Raspberry Fool mixture in the refrigerator for at least 30 minutes to allow the flavors to meld together.
6. Serve:
    - Spoon the chilled Honey Raspberry Fool into serving glasses or bowls. Garnish with fresh raspberries and mint leaves if desired.
7. Enjoy:
    - Serve immediately and enjoy this light and refreshing dessert with the delightful combination of honey and raspberries.

This Honey Raspberry Fool is perfect for a quick and elegant dessert that highlights the natural sweetness of honey and the vibrant flavor of raspberries. It's a versatile dessert that can be enjoyed year-round, and it's sure to impress your guests!

Honey Chocolate Chip Scones

Ingredients:

- 2 cups all-purpose flour
- 1/4 cup granulated sugar
- 1 tablespoon baking powder
- 1/2 teaspoon salt
- 1/2 cup (1 stick) unsalted butter, cold and cut into small pieces
- 1/2 cup chocolate chips (semi-sweet or milk chocolate)
- 1/2 cup milk (whole milk or any milk of your choice)
- 1/4 cup honey
- 1 teaspoon vanilla extract
- Optional: Additional honey for drizzling

Instructions:

1. Preheat Oven:
    - Preheat your oven to 400°F (200°C). Line a baking sheet with parchment paper or lightly grease it.
2. Prepare Dry Ingredients:
    - In a large bowl, whisk together the flour, sugar, baking powder, and salt.
3. Cut in Butter:
    - Add the cold butter pieces to the flour mixture. Use a pastry cutter or your fingertips to cut the butter into the flour until the mixture resembles coarse crumbs with pea-sized butter pieces.
4. Add Chocolate Chips:
    - Stir in the chocolate chips until evenly distributed.
5. Combine Wet Ingredients:
    - In a separate bowl, whisk together the milk, honey, and vanilla extract until well combined.
6. Mix Dough:
    - Pour the wet ingredients into the bowl with the dry ingredients. Stir gently with a fork or spatula until the dough just comes together. Avoid overmixing.
7. Form Scones:
    - Transfer the dough onto a lightly floured surface. Pat the dough into a circle or rectangle about 1-inch thick.
8. Cut Scones:
    - Use a sharp knife or a bench scraper to cut the dough into triangles or squares, about 8 pieces.
9. Bake:
    - Place the scones on the prepared baking sheet, leaving space between them. Bake in the preheated oven for 15-18 minutes, or until the scones are golden brown on top and cooked through.
10. Cool and Serve:

- Remove from the oven and let the scones cool on a wire rack. Drizzle with additional honey if desired.
11. Enjoy:
    - Serve these Honey Chocolate Chip Scones warm or at room temperature. They are delicious on their own or with a cup of tea or coffee.

These scones are best enjoyed fresh on the day they are made, but you can store leftovers in an airtight container at room temperature for up to 2 days. Warm them briefly in the oven or microwave before serving to refresh them.

www.ingramcontent.com/pod-product-compliance
Lightning Source LLC
LaVergne TN
LVHW081610060526
838201LV00054B/2178